Keats, Skepticism, and
the Religion of Beauty

Ronald A. Sharp

Keats, Skepticism, and the Religion of Beauty

The University of Georgia Press

Athens

Set in 10 on 13 point Caledonia type
Printed in the United States of America

Library of Congress Cataloging in Publication Data

Sharp, Ronald A
  Keats, skepticism, and the religion of beauty.
  Bibliography.
  Includes index.
    1. Keats, John, 1795–1821—Religion and ethics.
  2. Keats, John, 1795–1821—Aesthetics.   I. Title.
  PR4838.R4S5   821'.7   78-21463
                  ISBN 0-8203-0470-0

The publication of this book was supported in part
by a grant from the Andrew W. Mellon Foundation, administered by the American Council of
Learned Societies. The University of Georgia
Press gratefully acknowledges this assistance.

TO INESE
"green felicity"

What though I am not wealthy in the dower
Of spanning wisdom; though I do not know
The shiftings of the mighty winds that blow
Hither and thither all the changing thoughts
Of man: though no great minist'ring reason sorts
Out the dark mysteries of human souls
To clear conceiving: yet there ever rolls
A vast idea before me, and I glean
Therefrom my liberty; thence too I've seen
The end and aim of Poesy. 'Tis clear
As any thing most true; as that the year
Is made of the four seasons—manifest
As a large cross, some old cathedral's crest,
Lifted to the white clouds.

   John Keats, "Sleep and Poetry"

Contents

Acknowledgments

I am happy to acknowledge the kind assistance of friends, colleagues, students, and teachers who have helped to shape this book. E. D. Hirsch, Jr. provided invaluable guidance, criticism, and support at every stage of this project, from its inception in a seminar paper at the University of Virginia in 1973 and its development into a doctoral dissertation, through its final revisions as a completed book. For the gift of his wide learning, critical acumen, intellectual integrity, and patience, I feel the most intense gratitude.

I owe special thanks to those who gave generously of their time and talent by reading my manuscript and offering important suggestions: William P. Albrecht, Harold Bloom, James D. Boulger, George Core, Robert W. Daniel, Gerald Duff, Michael S. Harper, Robert Langbaum, Charles I. Patterson, Jr., and George Steiner. To Clifford Siskin and Frederick Turner, who also carefully read the manuscript and gave me invaluable advice, I owe the delight of long hours of conversation about Keats, from which I profited greatly, and the special joys of intellectual camaraderie.

I wish to thank Reed Browning, Robert Cantwell, Philip Church, Daniel Clift, Galbraith Crump, Joanne Diehl, Michael Gassenmeier, and Patrick Holland for their assistance and encouragement; Debbie Hamilton, James Hans, Eleanor Loucks, Suzanne Plybon, Mary Poovey, and Hope Weir for their help with typing and proofreading; Carol Ann McClish for compiling the index; Robert Buffington, Ellen Harris, Malcolm M. Mac-Donald, Karen Orchard, and Paul Zimmer of the University of Georgia Press for their patience and skill in turning a manuscript into a book; and John Rowlett, not least for his eagle editorial eye, but also for his penetrating criticism and his constant concern.

I am also indebted to my students at Kenyon College, in whose classrooms many of the arguments of this book grew to their final form. Bruce Haywood, provost of Kenyon College, provided generous support, as did the staff of Kenyon's Chalmers Memorial

ACKNOWLEDGMENTS

Library and, through a grant, the Kenyon Faculty Development Fund.

I would like to thank the *Explicator* and the *Kenyon Review* for permission to reprint some material in this book which first appeared in those publications. Unfortunately I cannot acknowledge the benefit of Jack Stillinger's edition of Keats. *The Poems of John Keats* (Harvard University Press, 1978) appeared while this volume was in press; my citations therefore are of necessity from earlier editions.

My deepest and warmest thanks go to my wife, Inese, whose tolerance, encouragement, and intelligent advice have persisted through every stage of my work. It would require a Keats to express my appreciation adequately.

Introduction

This book explains the relationship between Keats's courageous acceptance of human limitations on the one hand, and his magnificent sense of human possibilities on the other. Ever since Matthew Arnold identified a tough-minded "flint and iron"[1] in Keats's work alongside the more obvious tenderheartedness (the "versifying Pet-lamb,"[2] as Keats himself called it), critics have had to come to terms with these two essential qualities and their relationship. The distinction has been formulated in numerous ways: the real as against the ideal, the mortal as against the immortal, the earthly as against the transcendent, the skeptical as against the aesthetic, or the naturalistic as against the visionary. Yet for all the divergent and sometimes incompatible attempts to characterize these two impulses, there has, quite rightly, been widespread agreement that there really are two central impulses in Keats, and that understanding their exact nature and relationship is crucial to a clear understanding of his work as a whole.

The most common method of dealing with this problem has been to regard the impulses as conflicting. Douglas Bush, for example, sees at the center of Keats's work a "tension between the ideal and the actual [which] takes a variety of related forms," so that "even in his ripest maturity Keats . . . was continually divided against himself."[3] While Bush considers the conflict both pervasive and central throughout Keats's entire career, other critics, like Jack Stillinger, suggest that the tenderheartedness that predominates in the early poetry finally gives way to a genuine tough-mindedness as Keats moves away from his earlier trust in the vision-

1

ary imagination.[4] Both critics are attempting to explain the relationship of these two impulses, Bush with his model of permanent tension and Stillinger with his chronological schema. What they share—and this has become the most widely accepted view of Keats—is the assumption that the two impulses are not compatible, that they are fundamentally in conflict.

The major purpose of this book is to define these two essential impulses in Keats more accurately in order to demonstrate that, far from being in tension, they are perfectly compatible, and that the most accurate way of understanding their relationship is to view them not as elements in conflict but as problem and solution. The problem Keats faced, as I understand it, was both historical and personal: How can a religious and metaphysical skeptic find a source of endurance and affirmation in a world of unavoidable suffering? For the "flint and iron" in Keats is even tougher than we have recognized, and if we are to understand its relationship with the tenderhearted element in him, we must first of all recognize just how radical Keats's skepticism really is, and how pervasive is his insistence on the inevitability of suffering. Keats's solution to the problem posed by skepticism is what I shall be calling "aestheticism." It should be emphasized that I mean to suggest no associations whatever with the literary movement at the end of the nineteenth century that is also sometimes called by that name. What I have in mind, instead, is what Keats calls the "principle of beauty in all things" (*Letters*, 2:263), a principle of life and not just art that Keats intentionally offers as the foundation for a new kind of religion.[5] This tenderhearted element in Keats springs directly out of the tough-minded and it involves neither escape nor the visionary imagination, both of which Keats considered the bane of the first generation of romantics. Instead, Keats develops a fully humanized religion of beauty, paradoxically rooted in skepticism and offered as an alternative not to the inescapably painful world but to the Christian response to that world.[6]

Critics have largely ignored the religious concerns and implications of Keats's work, perhaps because they have believed, as Walter Jackson Bate has said, that "the poetry itself is so largely untouched by any direct interest in religion, either one way or another."[7] I shall be arguing quite the contrary, but I think the most important reason for the relative neglect stems from a fundamental misunderstanding of the nature and relationship of Keats's skepticism and aestheticism. I hope to show that the two issues—his religious concerns and the relationship between his skepticism and aestheticism—are intimately connected. Not only can we better understand the nature and relationship of Keats's two fundamental impulses by considering them in the context of his religious concerns, but once we understand that relationship we can also see just how central religious issues are to Keats's poetic enterprise. For it is no accident that Keats employs a religious vocabulary or framework in most of his major poems and letters. One has only to consider "Sleep and Poetry," *Endymion,* "The Eve of St. Agnes," "Ode to Psyche," "Ode on Melancholy," "Ode on a Grecian Urn," the two "Hyperion" poems, the "vale of Soul-making" or the "Mansion of Many Apartments" or the "finer tone" letters, to realize how pervasive such expressions are in Keats's work.

There is nothing unusual, of course, about discovering that a romantic poet uses religious language. One thinks, for example, of the final section of "Tintern Abbey," or of Byron's description of Don Juan and Haidée as

> By their own feelings *hallow'd* and united,
>   Their *priest* was Solitude, and they were wed:
> And they were happy, for to their young eyes
> Each was an *angel,* and earth *paradise.*
>   (*Don Juan,* 2. 204; emphasis mine.)

But what is significant in Keats's use of religious language is that it represents a sustained attempt to accommodate his untraditional but passionate religious feelings to readers who were unaccustomed to a conception of spirituality that does not depend on—that in fact denies—transcendent reality. Far from being merely ornamental or conventional, as most of his critics have assumed, Keats's religious language reflects a direct and intensive engagement with religious issues, an engagement that I believe is central to his work. In nearly every one of his major poems and letters Keats sets up a traditional religious framework which he then either contrasts with or appropriates to his own new and radically untraditional humanized religion.

The most sustained attempt to explore Keats's religious views is Robert Ryan's *Keats: the Religious Sense*, which appeared while the present book was undergoing its final revisions. Treating Keats's religious concerns developmentally, Ryan sketches the religious milieu in which Keats grew up, the contemporary theological issues and trends that would have been familiar to him, and the various influences that Keats's friends exerted upon his religious beliefs. But Ryan dwells almost exclusively on the letters, deliberately ignoring the major poems which, he says, with one or two exceptions do "not concern [themselves] in any obvious or direct way with modern religious themes." It seems to me an extraordinary act of omission to preclude a poet's poems from a consideration of his religious views, particularly when those poems do concern themselves with crucial religious themes, which may not be "obvious or direct" precisely because they are so "modern." But Ryan denies that Keats was "an early exponent of modern secular humanism" or "an agnostic." "The general nature of his belief," according to Ryan, "belonged to a fairly old tradition in English religious thought: the tradition of natural religion."[8] Though I disagree with Ryan's conclusions, I think he is right to emphasize Keats's serious involvement with religious concerns. By exploring the connections between the poems and the letters, and by considering the implications of Keats's religious views for an understanding of his larger vision, I shall attempt to demonstrate that a proper understanding of Keats's religious attitudes alters one's interpretation of the whole body of his work.[9]

To the extent that Keats's poetry and letters demonstrate an acute awareness of the skeptical legacy of the Enlightenment and reveal a complex and fully developed response to the problem of religious faith, they can fruitfully be regarded as part of that process of progressive secularization which, as M. H. Abrams has reemphasized in *Natural Supernaturalism*, was central to the romantic period.[10] But unlike Blake or Wordsworth or Coleridge, Keats maintained a deep and abiding skepticism about the possibility of knowing with certainty any kind of transcendent or higher reality. For Keats the imagination was an exclusively human agency serving purely human ends. Its religious function was not to mediate a holy communion with higher reality but to endow human life with beauty, which he regarded as holy not because it was part of some grand scheme of things, but simply because it made life worth living. That, in fact, is precisely what Keats meant by *beauty:* that which is life-affirming. He was extraordinarily self-conscious about his historical position "in these days so far retir'd / From happy pieties."[11] From the beginning, in fact, Keats understood that the real challenge of surpassing his predecessors' poetry was to do so without either the relative metaphysical certainty or the traditional religious support that had provided the basis of almost all the great English poetry of the past—including, even if in a new transformation, that of the early romantics.

If it is true, as I have suggested, that the most accurate way of viewing the relationship between Keats's skepticism and aestheticism is to see the latter as the solution to the problems posed by the former, it might seem that I have merely reversed Stillinger's chronological schema. But that is not the case, since Keats very early saw not just the problem but the solution as well. Hence, even in his earliest poems and letters we find a kind of spiritual equilibrium, a characteristically Keatsian balance of both the limitations and the possibilities of life and poetry. There is neither a persistent conflict between Keats's two essential impulses nor any essential change of outlook. The "vast idea" which he so ecstatically seized upon in "Sleep and Poetry," written in 1816 when he was only twenty-one years old, involves a guiding conception of human life, and of the role of poetry based on that view of life. Although I disagree with John Middleton Murry's interpretation of the vast idea, I fully accept his description of its place in Keats's development. After "Sleep and Poetry," Murry says, "what was to follow of Keats' life and work was a further realization, a 'proving upon his pulses' of the idea of which he already had intuitive possession. He lived, thought, felt, imagined and wrote himself into it more fully, but it was already his."[12]

In claiming a high degree of substantive consistency for Keats's work, I do not wish to imply that his early work is as fully realized or as brilliant as his later work. But I think it is a serious mistake to read the early work condescendingly. No one can doubt that Keats's early poetry betrays occasional uncertainties, or that in general it suffers remarkably by comparison with his later work. But it is another matter altogether to regard the early poetry as the product of a poet whose deepest convictions about life and poetry have yet to mature. Without denying the rich variety of his work, and without trivializing his continual struggle to rethink his most fundamental conceptions of life and poetry, I would suggest that Keats's later work confirms the view of life presented in the early work, and reaffirms the validity of the poetic program outlined in "Sleep and Poetry." Keats's poetry and letters reveal a coherence and spiritual integrity which, even though they achieve their fullest expression in the later work, are readily apparent in the early work as well. Consequently, in the discussions that follow, I shall move freely not only between the letters and the poems, but back and forth from the early Keats to the late.

But I do not wish to suggest that Keats was a scrupulously systematic thinker. Particularly in the letters, he usually provides only hints of his most profound ideas rather than full-scale explanations. Nor would one expect Keats to offer elaborate explications of his speculations, since he thought the most immediate proof of them lay not in rational analysis but in experience ("axioms in philosophy are not axioms until they are proved upon our pulses" [*Letters*, 1:279]) or through the imagination ("What the imagination seizes as Beauty must be truth" [*Letters*, 1:184]). But Keats never denied that systematic thinking could arrive at the truth, by which he means human and not metaphysical truth. "I have never yet," he tells Bailey, "been able to perceive how any thing can be known for truth by consequitive reasoning— *and yet it must be*" (*Letters*, 1:185; emphasis mine).

My technique in this book will be to reconstruct the view of life and poetry that Keats gives us unsystematically in his poems and letters. To do so, I shall frequently venture behind the poems and letters, piecing together the pattern of assumptions that gives them their extraordinary consistency. Keats's work is itself the best available proof that one need not proceed systematically in order to be consistent. But the function of critical interpretation is not the same as the function of poetry, and if we wish to understand the complexities of Keats's individual works, it will be best to try to see them in their consistent relationship with the coherent view of life and art that underlies them.

I am intent on opening up the question of Keats's achievement at exactly that level where critical agreement has been purchased at the price of condescension towards Keats. As high as his reputation is, and as fine as his best critics have been, Keats still is the object of what to my mind is an unjustified condescension. This book, while it disagrees with Middleton Murry's conclusions about Keats's religion, takes its bearings from Murry's conviction that Keats's religious concerns are central to his work, and "that an attitude of condescension or patronage towards him is utterly impossible. . . . The proper attitude of criticism towards Keats is one of complete humility."[13] In 1949, some twenty years after making this remark, Murry felt the need to reiterate it. "I am certain of one thing," he said, "that our appreciation of the significance of Keats, which has so greatly grown in the hundred years since Monckton Milnes first published the *Life and Letters,* has still far to go before it is commensurate with what he really was."[14] As much as our understanding and appreciation of Keats has grown again in the last quarter century, no one has thought it necessary to challenge the widely held assumption that Keats's two essential impulses are conflicting. This book attempts to do just that, but whether it can lay claim to anything beyond novelty must be determined by judging the validity of the arguments that follow.

I

The Problem: Skepticism

Keats's anticlericalism and his frequent allusions to the "pious frauds of Religion" (*Letters*, 2:80) are too widely known for anyone to dispute his antipathy to Christianity.[1] Benjamin Bailey, with whom he discoursed at great length about such matters, contends that Keats "was no scoffer, & in no sense was he an infidel"; but he reports, in the same passage of his recollections, that Keats had confessed "his sceptical nature in all things."[2] Bailey interprets this confession as an exaggeration, but notwithstanding Keats's fiery dedication to poetry, it seems to me perfectly accurate.

The story of Keats bowing to the figure of Voltaire which Haydon had included in his huge canvas as an example of an unbeliever, reveals a good deal more than Keats's remarkable sense of the comic. For the influence of Voltaire on Keats and his intellectual milieu was, as Stuart Sperry has demonstrated, considerably more pervasive than had been previously recognized. Sperry argues that there is a close resemblance between Keats and Voltaire in their vision of man as a predominantly natural creature in a world of suffering; in their "distrust of formalized religion and its consolations as the outgrowth of superstition and human need rather than of divine authority"; and in their conception of history as a struggle between man and "savagery, superstition, and tyranny." Even the famous phrase "pious frauds of Religion" is almost a literal translation from Voltaire's *Dictionnaire philosophique* and *Essai sur les moeurs et l'esprit des nations:* "S'il faut user de fraudes pieuses avec le peuple."[3]

But the extent of Voltaire's influence on Keats concerns

9

me less than the extent of Keats's skepticism. Robert Gittings is surely right when he suggests that Keats "could not be satisfied with a complete and negative scepticism" such as Voltaire's. "Somewhere," Gittings says, Keats "must find a faith."[4] But the nature of that faith, which Keats refers to as "a recourse somewhat human" (*Letters*, 1:179), is intimately related to and circumscribed by the skepticism, and before we take up the nature of Keats's new faith, we need to consider just how deep the current of skepticism runs in him.[5]

———

"You," Keats tells Bailey, "have all your Life (I think so) believed every Body—I have suspected every Body" (*Letters*, 1:292). "Axioms in philosophy are not axioms," he writes to Reynolds, "until they are proved upon our pulses" (*Letters*, 1:279). Echoing the same sentiment a year later, he writes to his brother and sister-in-law: "Nothing ever becomes real till it is experienced—Even a Proverb is no proverb to you till your Life has illustrated it" (*Letters*, 2:81). In that same long letter, written at the height of his creative powers, he confesses: "I am however young writing at random—straining at particles of light in the midst of a great darkness—without knowing the bearing of any one assertion of any one opinion" (*Letters*, 2:80). To accept the full implications of this last statement would be tantamount to charging Keats with an inconsistency and naiveté of which he is emphatically not guilty. But there is an important kernel of truth in what he says, and that it is related to his radical skepticism seems to me confirmed by two of his sonnets, "Written Upon the Top of Ben Nevis" and "Why Did I Laugh To-night?" In both of these poems the poet finds himself condemned to a bleak vision of despair arising largely out of his inability to understand highest things. "O Darkness!" he cries in "Why Did I Laugh To-night?": "Darkness!

ever must I moan, / To question Heaven and Hell and Heart in vain" (lines 7–8). "Written Upon the Top of Ben Nevis" also suggests man's inability to comprehend heaven or hell, and its conclusion constitutes a significant reversal of the tradition of mountain-top revelations:

> Even so vague is man's sight of himself!
>   Here are the craggy stones beneath my feet,—
> Thus much I know that, a poor witless elf,
>   I tread on them,—that all my eye doth meet
> Is mist and crag, not only on this height,
> But in the world of thought and mental might!
> (lines 9–14)

There is no breakthrough in this poem, no sudden illumination of ultimate reality such as Wordsworth discovers, for example, through the mists on Mount Snowden. Unlike Wordsworth or Coleridge, Keats could never commit himself to a confident belief in a "something far more deeply interfused" ("Tintern Abbey," line 96) which the creative imagination could apprehend. He understood the human desire for such a reality, but any certainty in the matter, any suggestion that one could trust, as Wordsworth and Coleridge did, that the insights of the imagination were genuine metaphysical truths, Keats firmly rejected.

I think it is important that we bear this in mind when we encounter interpretations of Keats's work which assume that he did, in fact, have a metaphysics, by which I mean not just an attitude towards reality but a belief in some sort of higher reality.[6] Ignoring Keats's skepticism, Earl Wasserman brilliantly constructs an elaborate metaphysics out of the fragmentary speculations in Keats's letters and then proceeds to interpret the poetry within that framework. There is, of course, nothing wrong with using the letters in the interpretation of the poems; Wasserman is quite right to insist on the value of doing so. He is also right to search for a principle of coherence that gives Keats's work its distinctive shape and direction—a "frame of reference,"[7] as he calls it—in terms of which the individual poems can be better understood. Wasserman's error, in my judgment, is that he fails to recognize that the frame of reference in which Keats is working precludes metaphysics, and that, although Keats does have a distinctive view of reality, he is at great pains to obviate the whole issue of ultimate or metaphysical reality. So far as I can tell, Keats never had either a consistent metaphysics or any serious interest in developing one.[8]

Nor was it merely a skepticism about the visionary imagination that made Keats suspicious about confidently knowing metaphysical truth. He was no more confident about the procedure of logical analysis. "Now my dear fellow," he writes to Bailey, "I must once for all tell you I have not one Idea of the truth of any of my speculations—I shall never be a Reasoner" (*Letters*, 1:243). The famous theory of Negative Capability, like the refrain in "What the Thrush Said" ("O fret not after knowledge—I have none"), argues against "any irritable reaching after fact & reason" on the grounds that such an active pursuit can only be fruitless (*Letters*, 1:193). "Things cannot to the will / Be settled," Keats says in the verse epistle "To J. H. Reynolds, Esq.," "but they tease us out of thought" (lines 76–77).

C. E. Pulos scarcely exaggerates when he calls skepticism "the most important intellectual problem of . . . the age of romanticism." In *Religion and the Rise of Scepticism* Franklin L. Baumer argues that in the "phase of the sceptical tradition . . . which coincided with the Enlightenment and the French Revolution . . . , the big new thing to note is the profound shift of consciousness from the theistic to the humanistic plane." M. H. Abrams has elaborately documented that shift, focusing on the various ways in which romantic poets and philosophers secularized religion. "The general tendency," he says, "was, in diverse degrees and ways, to naturalize the supernatural and to humanize the divine." But Abrams also recognizes that the purpose of the secularization was "to save . . . the cardinal values of their religious heritage, by reconstituting them in a way that would make them intellectually acceptable, as well as emotionally pertinent, for the time being."[9] For all their secularizing transformations and reinterpretations of Christianity, Blake and Wordsworth and Coleridge continued to believe in a higher reality. Although Abrams quite rightly assumes that Keats shares with the other major romantics this involvement in a religious and epistemological crisis, Abrams does not, I think, recognize that Keats's skepticism in this regard distinguishes him from the first generation romantics in a still more significant way.

Keats seems to have understood the humanizing implications of Wordworth's immanentism, but he also seems to have understood that the immanentism went hand in hand, for Wordsworth, with a belief in transcendent reality. "However deeply interfused in the processes of nature [Wordsworth] may have felt God to be," says Willard Sperry, "his doctrine of God made full place for the divine transcendence as well as immanence."[10] Sperry then quotes a passage from book 6 of *The Prelude*, which even in the 1805 edition contains more pure supernaturalism than natural supernaturalism:

> the one
> Surpassing Life, which out of space and time,
> Nor touch'd by welterings of passion, is
> And hath the name of God.
> (lines 154–57)

Keats recognized that Wordsworth had joined in an important process of secularization, and in his famous comparison of Wordsworth and Milton he applauds Wordsworth for seeing more deeply into the human heart than Milton had. But Keats also realized that Wordsworth shared as much with Milton as he did with Keats. What Wordsworth shared with Milton was the belief that there was a reality that transcended this world, and it is this belief that defines "traditional religion," as I shall be using the phrase throughout this book, and distinguishes it from Keats's fully humanized religion.[11]

A truly radical skeptic like Keats can never rest with a blanket denial of the existence of God. "You know my ideas about Religion," Keats writes to Bailey in 1818: "I do not think myself more in the right than other people and . . . nothing in this world is proveable" (*Letters*, 1:242). There is, to be sure, a certain amount of Shelleyan disgust with and mocking of the abuses of the established church in Keats's work, and also a rather pervasive sense of the obsolescence, naiveté, and superstition of Christianity. But Keats's critique of traditional religion is more often characterized by nostalgia than by condemnation. Consistent with his belief that nothing is provable, Keats is usually cautious in his denials, and always careful to indicate not that there definitely is no higher reality or that it cannot possibly be known, but that any certainty in such matters is impossible. It should come as no surprise, then, that Keats does occasionally refer to God or immortality as though they did in fact exist. Any argument for Keats's agnosticism which sweeps these instances under the rug not only lacks integrity but misses the spirit of his skepticism. For Keats was no mere scoffer: his skepticism was radical enough to allow him to speculate upon occasion about metaphysical matters without ever for a moment assuming that any certainty was possible.

Concern with the limits of knowledge is of course most stringently applied by Keats to a critique not of dogmatic atheism but of traditional religion, which assumes a certainty to which he finds it impossible to consent. Religion in the romantic period had not yet received, as A. S. P. Woodhouse has pointed out, the two additionally severe blows that it would be dealt in the Victorian period: the Darwinian thesis about nature and the critical study of Scripture.[12] But Keats's attitude towards religion was already essentially that of the modern historical relativist, who sees all myths and religions as purely human phenomena—not as true or false but as so many attempts to give meaning to human life. As the myth becomes less functional, it gradually dies, as one of Keats's many sardonic comments about the Christian clergy suggests: "Parsons will always keep up their Character," he writes to George and Georgiana, "but as it is said there are some animals, the Ancients knew, which we do not; let us hope our posterity will miss the black badger with tri-cornered hat; Who knows but some Revisor of Buffon or Pliny, may put an account of the parson in the Appendix; No one will then believe it any more than we believe in the Phoenix" (*Letters*, 2:70). This comment represents consider-ably more than a critique of institutional abuses in the church; together with Keats's other views of religion, it both prophesies and approves the demise of Christianity.

Indeed, for all intents and purposes Keats already viewed Christianity as just another myth—a happy piety of the past on the same level, and doomed to the same fate of gradual extinction, as the myth of the Titans in "Hyperion." In that poem, whose central allegory assumes a skeptical and his-toricist reduction of all myths or ideologies, Keats dramatizes this historical process by which one divine myth is super-seded by a newer, more human one. W. K. C. Guthrie, re-ferring not to Keats's poem but to what he regards as the most plausible interpretation of Zeus's mythological usurpa-tion, tells us that "the Titans were indeed of an older gen-eration in Greece, and their defeat reflects the fruitless opposition offered by the older religion to that of the new-comers."[13] One has only to compare the early sonnet "Written in Disgust of Vulgar Superstition" to realize that Keats was concerned very early with the issue of old, outworn faiths being replaced by newer, more humanistic ones:

> The church bells toll a melancholy round,
>   Calling the people to some other prayers,
>   Some other gloominess, more dreadful cares,
> More hearkening to the sermon's horrid sound.
> Surely the mind of man is closely bound
>   In some black spell; seeing that each one tears
>   Himself from fireside joys, and Lydian airs,
> And converse high of those with glory crown'd.
> Still, still they toll, and I should feel a damp—
>   A chill as from a tomb, did I not know
> That they are dying like an outburnt lamp;
>   That 'tis their sighing, wailing ere they go
>   Into oblivion;—that fresh flowers will grow,
> And many glories of immortal stamp.

I quote the entire poem because, although its critique of Christianity is harsher than the rather nostalgic critique of the Titans in "Hyperion," it takes its bearings from the same conception of religion. Keats represents Christianity in this sonnet as a phenomenon which has had its day and now is sinking into oblivion. Not surprisingly, most critics have glossed over the significance of this poem. It was, as we know, written in only fifteen minutes and Keats never published it. Nor can one quarrel with the unanimous judgment of those critics who have dealt with the poem: it is relatively weak. But the more revealing reason for slighting this sonnet is the apparent assumption that the poem has little substantive interest, that it somehow does not fall into the mainstream of Keats's thought or development.

Bate passes the poem off as "naive," an instance of "the youthful, almost absent-minded agnosticism with which [Keats] began his adult life . . . the product of sheer accident and environment," and of the influence of Shelley and Hunt.[14] Gittings merely reiterates the influence of Shelley

16

and Hunt and points to the fact that the poem was written hastily. Amy Lowell insists that "it was no agnostic who wrote *Written in Disgust of Vulgar Superstition*"; Douglas Bush claims that the poem is "unwontedly anti-Christian"; and Robert Ryan, who devotes more space to the poem than anyone else, tries to soften its impact by claiming that the phrase "vulgar superstition," which does in fact "describe Christianity itself," was "widely used by exponents of natural religion."[15] The other critics who explore Keats's religious views in some depth (Middleton Murry, H. N. Fairchild, James Benziger, and Newell F. Ford) omit any mention of the poem at all in their various studies of Keats.[16]

Yet "Written in Disgust of Vulgar Superstition" seems to me perfectly consistent with Keats's attitude toward traditional religion throughout his career. It may be shriller in tone and more self-righteous in posture than is usually the case with Keats's treatment of Christianity, but in at least two important ways it is typical. There is, first of all, the underlying historical awareness of the situation of religion in the modern world and the implication that Christianity can no longer adequately fulfill human needs. Second, there is in the final image of the poem, the "fresh flowers" that "will grow," the implication that a new alternative to traditional religion will arise, an alternative that is closely associated with poetry ("many glories of immortal stamp").

Douglas Bush has noticed the importance of this association, and he has even suggested that "the positive interest of the sonnet is in Keats's assumption that the only religion is poetry."[17] But it seems to me remarkable that Bush would allow such a bold and pregnant claim to remain unexplained. For on the face of it, the statement might well suggest that Keats's position in this sonnet is not unlike that attributed to him more generally by the Pre-Raphaelites and Aesthetes— a kind of art for art's sake position which Bush himself, like most modern critics, rightly discredits.[18] It is not enough merely to observe the association between religion and poetry without inquiring into the exact nature of the new religious function which Keats conceives for poetry and determining how central it is to his other major concerns.[19] That is among the subjects of the next two chapters, but before turning to Keats's solution to the problem of skepticism we must first examine the problem itself more closely.

I have already suggested that Keats's occasional references to God and immortality indicate a skepticism that precludes any kind of dogmatism or absolute certainty about metaphysical matters, even dogmatic atheism. But these few instances do not essentially alter one's overwhelming impression that Keats rejected traditional religion, as I have defined it. Indeed, a number of Keats's references to Christianity and immortality seem most accurately explained precisely in terms of the skepticism that underlies so much of his thought.

We see this most dramatically during Keats's illness in 1820, when he writes to Brown: "Is there another Life? Shall I awake and find all this a dream? There must be we cannot be created for this sort of suffering" (*Letters*, 2:346). This is the comment not of a faithful believer in immortality but of a man who, in the same spirit, had written to Fanny Brawne a few months earlier: "I long to believe in immortality" (*Letters*, 2:293).

Even as he lay sweating and delirious on his deathbed at Rome, Keats rejected Christianity, despite his painful awareness that he was thereby denying himself the comfort that comes with belief in an afterlife. When he told Severn, "I cannot believe in your book—the Bible,"[20] he was venting the same kind of bitterness that characterized many of his attitudes and relations in the last month. Nonetheless, this statement to Severn reflects not a temporary, tortured distortion, but a perfectly representative view of Keats's attitude to Christianity throughout his career. Severn took great comfort in believing that Keats had "died a Christian"[21] (a view which scarcely any scholars now share), and Bailey took equal delight in discovering whatever evidence he could for his conviction that Keats was no infidel. He was thus especially pleased to read the following words of Keats, written to George and Georgiana just after Tom's death: "the common observations of the commonest people on death are as true as their proverbs. I have scarce a doubt of immortality of some nature o[r] other" (*Letters*, 2:4).[22] Yet even in this statement one detects uncertainty ("of some nature o[r] other") along with the very real possibility that Keats was trying to console his brother and sister-in-law in a time of sorrow. But even if we are willing to consider the sentiment utterly sincere, we must remember that it was written after Keats had suffered a severe personal loss; in any case, it is by itself scarcely proof of anything like a firm belief in immortality.

Some of Keats's most striking references to immortality are really quite comic in nature. Beginning a long overdue letter to Reynolds in 1818, Keats apologizes for the lapse in his correspondence and playfully suggests that "the most unhappy hours in our lives are those in which we recollect times past to our own blushing—If we are immortal that must be the Hell—If I must be immortal, I hope it will be after having taken a little of 'that watery labyrinth' in order to forget some of my schoolboy days & others since those" (*Letters*, 1:273). A subtler ironic perspective on immortality is offered in the famous "finer tone" letter to Bailey, in which Keats outlines "another favorite Speculation of mine" (*Letters*, 1:185), whose irony seems to have escaped a critic as perceptive as Earl Wasserman. "We shall enjoy ourselves here after," says Keats, "by having what we called happiness on Earth repeated in a finer tone" (*Letters*, 1:185). This is indeed a peculiar notion of immortality which suggests that the afterlife will be just like earthly happiness, only in a finer tone. It is a version of heaven which is purposefully contrived to undermine the aspiration for a blissful afterlife as compensation for a mortal life of sorrow. In a discussion of the afterlife it is more than a little ironic that Keats emphasizes not the world of immortality but of mortality. For if there *is* an afterlife, he suggests, the degree of happiness one can expect in heaven will be determined precisely by the degree of happiness one achieves in life. If there is to be a final pie in the sky, it must be mixed and baked and sampled on earth, for although the taste may be finer in heaven, no new ingredients will be added there that have not already been included on earth.

Keats offers this "favorite Speculation" rather playfully, somewhat in the manner of the opening and closing quatrain of "Lines on the Mermaid Tavern":

> Souls of Poets dead and gone,
> What Elysium have ye known,
> Happy field or mossy cavern,
> Choicer than the Mermaid Tavern?
> (lines 1–4, 23–26)

But Keats is not being altogether frivolous in the "finer tone" letter. In his suggestion that if there is an afterlife one can best prepare for it by achieving happiness in this world, Keats characteristically lays his emphasis on the world of human actuality. In the statement immediately following his speculation that we shall enjoy ourselves hereafter in a finer tone, he says that "such a fate can only befall those who delight in sensation rather than hunger . . . after Truth." Keats is assuming here that higher truth cannot be known with any certainty, and it is this kind of epistemological skepticism that, in the "finer tone" letter as elsewhere, leads him to regard the immediate world as the only realm of experience about which man can be confident in his knowledge, and thus the most appropriate arena for man's spiritual aspirations. Only a month later Keats was to formulate the implications of this position in his letter about Negative Capability, in which the caveat to avoid "any irritable reaching after fact & reason" is based on the same skeptical assumption that the province of metaphysical reality is inevitably one of "uncertainties, Mysteries, doubts" (*Letters*, 1:193).[23] Charles Patterson has stated that Keats considered the immediate world "the sphere in which man finds the only true spirituality he will ever know."[24]

It is because Keats believes that the human is the true sphere of spirituality that he makes Apollo "die into life" at the end of "Hyperion" (3. 130), and has Endymion, who earlier had pursued the specter of happiness beyond this world, ultimately reject his desire for transcendence. In the "vale of Soul-making" letter Keats makes it equally clear that suffering cannot be justified on the assumption that it will be rewarded in some afterworld; suffering is shown to offer its own rewards in this world itself. Like the "finer tone" passage, which treats the religious question of immortality, the "vale of Soul-making" letter deals with still another religious issue, suffering and salvation. In both cases Keats rejects all theodicy in favor of a radical humanization, which considers dangerously deceptive any scheme that blinks—or even transcends—human suffering. "None can usurp this height," Moneta tells Keats in *The Fall of Hyperion*, "But those to whom the miseries of the world / Are misery, and will not let them rest" (1. 147–49).

Keats was rarely so despairing as to believe that no degree of happiness at all was available to man, but he did consider human life something that "must be undergone" (*Letters*, 1:293). "Such is this World," he writes to Bailey as early as 1817, "and we live . . . in a continual struggle against the suffocation of accidents" (*Letters*, 1:179). Young men gradually come to realize, he tells Taylor, that "Uneasiness" is "an habitual sensation, a pannier which is to weigh upon them through life" (*Letters*, 1:270). "There are enough real distresses and evils in wait for every one," he tells his sister, "to try the most vigorous health" (*Letters*, 2:329–30). Even "in the very temple of Delight," Keats says in "Ode on Melancholy," "Veil'd Melancholy has her sovran shrine" (lines 25–26). In "Ode to a Nightingale" he speaks of a world in which "men sit and hear each other groan" (line 24), and in the verse epistle "To J. H. Reynolds, Esq." he describes the horrifying clarity with which he "saw too distinct into the core / Of an eternal fierce destruction" (lines 96–97).

One cannot emphasize enough the frequency with which such sentiments occur throughout the whole range, from beginning to end, of Keats's poems and letters and the importance they hold for our understanding of Keats's rejection of any system or form of belief which would evade or transcend suffering. "Pleasure is oft a visitant," says Endymion, "but pain / Clings cruelly to us" (1. 906–7). "Scanty the hour," Keats says in "Lines Written in the Highlands," "and few the steps beyond the bourn of care" (line 29). Like the myth of the two urns in the final book of the *Iliad*,[25] these lines make it clear that the lot of man may be sometimes overwhelmingly full of sorrow and sometimes a mixture of happiness and sorrow, but it will never be a life of pure happiness unalloyed with suffering.

The "vale of Soul-making" passage, which contains Keats's most famous insistence on the inevitability of suffering, must be read in the context of what precedes it in the long journal letter to George and Georgiana. "This is the world—," he tells them, "thus we cannot expect to give way many hours to pleasure—Circumstances are like Clouds continually gathering and bursting—While we are laughing the seed of some trouble is put into . . . the wide arable land of events" (*Letters*, 2:79). A bit later he says: "I wonder how people exist with all their worries" (*Letters*, 2:83). Finally, just before launching into the discussion of soul-making, Keats says that he has recently been reading "two very different books":

Robertson's [History of] America and Voltaire's Siecle
De Louis xiv. . . . In How lementabl[e] a case do we
see the great body of the people in both instances: in
the first, where Men might seem to inherit quiet of
Mind from unsophisticated senses; from uncontamina-
tion of civilisation; and especially from their being as it
were estranged from the mutual helps of Society and
its mutual injuries—and thereby more immediately under the Protection of Providence—even there they had
mortal pains to bear as bad; or even worse than Baliffs,
Debts and Poverties of civilised Life—The whole appears to resolve into this—that Man is originally 'a poor
forked creature' subject to the same mischances as the
beasts of the forest, destined to hardships and disquietude of some kind or other. If he improves by degrees his bodily accomodations and comforts—at each
stage, at each accent there are waiting for him a fresh
set of annoyances.   (*Letters*, 2:100–101)

This is an extraordinary passage, not least of all because,
in its trenchant analysis of primitivism and civilization alike,
it represents a basic departure from early romanticism. In
both instances—the polished civilization of Louis XIV and
the primitive society of early America—man must bear "mortal pains" and suffer "hardships and disquietude of some
kind or other." As far as his essential happiness is concerned,
it matters little whether man "improves by degrees his bodily
accomodations and comforts," for at each stage new problems await him, "annoyances" which, Keats says a few sen-
tences later, "are as native to the world" as man:

The most interesting question that can come before us
is, How far by the persevering endeavours of a seldom
appearing Socrates Mankind may be made happy—I
can imagine such happiness carried to an extreme—but
what must it end in?—Death—and who could in such
a case bear with death—the whole troubles of life which
are now frittered away in a series of years, would the[n]
be accumulated for the last days of a being who instead
of hailing its approach, would leave this world as Eve

left Paradise—But in truth I do not at all believe in this sort of perfectibility—the nature of the world will not admit of it—the inhabitants of the world will correspond to itself—Let the fish philosophise the ice away from the Rivers in winter time and they shall be at continual play in the tepid delight of summer. Look at the Poles and at the sands of Africa, Whirlpools and volcanoes—Let men exterminate them and I will say that they may arrive at earthly Happiness—The point at which Man may arrive is as far as the paralel state in inanimate nature and no further.   (*Letters*, 2:101)

How fundamentally different is this view of human possibility from that of the early Shelley, for example. Keats emphatically denies the Godwinian assumption of human perfectibility. Suffering is too permanent a part of the human condition to allow for the possibility of any extensive happiness; therefore, political or social conditions, whether the civilization of Louis XIV or the primitivism of America, can never fundamentally alter the prospect of suffering which man faces. Keats reifies, as the Marxists would say, the law of necessity, and thus denies the possibility that any kind of social change could materially alter the harsh facts of human suffering. Even if one could imagine an extreme state of happiness, one would realize that it must end in death, and that one would therefore simply concentrate one's suffering in one's final days, since one "would leave this world as Eve left Paradise"—sadly, reluctantly. But it is the very "nature of the world" that "will not admit" of any conception of life as Paradise. One need only compare Wordsworth to see how far away Keats is from that poet's early belief in the possibility of making Paradise "a simple produce of the common day."[26]

Together with his religious and metaphysical skepticism, Keats's pervasive sense of the inevitability of suffering obviously imposed severe limitations on the possibilities open to both man and poetry. To ground human happiness in a theodicy that explains away suffering thus becomes as illusory as grounding happiness in the possibility of perfectibility, as the early Shelley does. For to the extent that both positions promise man more than is possible, they deceive him, as Endymion is deceived in the early part of his journey, and ultimately they deposit man forlorn and disillusioned, like the weary knight in "La Belle Dame sans Merci," on the cold hillside of reality. As Keats tells us in *The Fall of Hyperion*, such illusions are the products of dreamers, and "The poet and the dreamer are distinct, / Diverse, sheer opposite, antipodes" (1. 199–200). For true poets, "the miseries of the world / Are misery, and will not let them rest" (1. 148–49).

The "vale of Soul-making" passage must be read as Keats's solution to the traditional religious problems of suffering and mortality. He says explicitly in that letter that he is sketching "a system of Salvation which does not affront our reason and humanity—I am convinced that many difficulties which christians labour under would vanish before it" (*Letters*, 2:103). After thus establishing his antipathy to any solution that slights the human realities of suffering and death, or transfigures them in some divine scheme, Keats outlines a system of salvation which he sets in direct opposition to the Christian alternative. Like the Christian system, Keats's both assumes a world of suffering and argues its necessity: "Do you not see how necessary a World of Pains and troubles is to school an Intelligence and make it a Soul?" (*Letters*, 2:102). But unlike the Christian, Keats (with his characteristic insistence on human immediacy) justifies suffering on the grounds that we will be rewarded not in some afterworld but in this world, the only one we can certainly know.

The nature of that reward is intimately related to Keats's whole resolution of the problems posed by his radical skepticism and his conception of human life as invariably full of sorrow. Before returning to this crucial letter on the vale of soul-making, we shall find it helpful to explain the fundamental principle of that resolution, which I call aestheticism, in some detail, for the major portion of Keats's energies was directed not towards establishing the limitations of knowledge, of belief, and of happiness, but towards fashioning the kinds of alternatives, the kinds of responses to these unalterable facts, which might offer some consolation in a world in which the old gods are forever dead.

II

The Solution: Aestheticism

If suffering is inevitable and cannot be justified on the basis of a faith in some higher scheme of things, why do men continue to live? This is a question which Keats struggled with throughout his life, and it seems fair to say that the most salient characteristic of his personal life was the continual effort to come to grips with the suffering and death that had been a daily reality for him since childhood. That his "vast idea" and his poetry and letters can also be viewed as a heroic response to this experience no one can doubt. But neither can one doubt that Keats's concern with suffering and death extends beyond his own experience. Near the end of his life, the agony of his illness created a strong temptation to commit suicide, but none of Keats's biographers has doubted that he had considered it earlier, even before he was sick. Although Keats had experienced an extraordinary amount of suffering for any man, let alone one so young, it is no more accurate to regard his flirtations with suicide as merely the result of "the bluedevil temperament" (*Letters*, 2:356) or his own personal troubles than it is to suggest that he considered suffering inevitable in human affairs only because he had himself suffered so much. Whatever grounds for affirmation Keats discovered were wrested out of an unending battle against despair. "We live . . . in a continual struggle against the suffocation of accidents," he had written to Bailey as early as November 1817 (*Letters*, 1:179), so that if he were to find a source of hope it must be one that never blinked the reality of suffering or violated his deep and abiding skepticism.

The best gloss to Keats's resolution of these problems occurs in this same early letter. Bailey was soon to be ordained and had just been denied a curacy at Lincoln, apparently in a rather underhanded manner. After railing against the clergy in what was to become his accustomed fashion, Keats draws the following conclusion:

> Such is this World—and we live . . . in a continual struggle against the suffocation of accidents—we must bear (and my Spleen is mad at the thought thereof) the Proud Mans Contumely—O for a recourse somewhat human independant of the great Consolations of Religion and undepraved Sensations. of the Beautiful. the poetical in all things—O for a Remedy against such wrongs within the pale of the world! . . . Would not earthly thing[s] do? By Heavens my dear Bailey, I know you have a spice of what I mean. . . . The thought that we are mortal makes us groan.   (*Letters*, 1:179)

As he often does in his letters, Keats begins by addressing himself to a specific situation or event and then proceeds to the more general issues that it raises. In this brief passage we find the central ideas which formed the foundation for his vision of the world and the function of poetry within it.

Because he could not accept any version of the Christian theodicy, Keats sought a "recourse . . . *independant* of the great Consolations of Religion" (emphasis mine). Any consolation must be grounded not on metaphysical or otherworldly principles but on "earthly thing[s]," and it must, he says, be based on "the Beautiful. the poetical in all things." That is to say, in place of the "pious frauds of Religion," Keats offers the alternative of beauty as a more satisfactory consolation. But beauty is offered as an alternative not to the actual world (as critics who consider Keats's aestheticism escapist would have us believe) but to the Christian response to that world. Aestheticism and traditional religion are variant modes of consolation in a world which, according to both positions, is essentially painful and difficult to endure.

But what exactly does Keats mean by beauty? If it is true,

as I have suggested, that Keats was very skeptical about all metaphysical matters, it follows that beauty must not have an abstract or metaphysical significance for Keats, but a human and functional one. With the exception of the famous beauty-truth equation in "Ode on a Grecian Urn," we search Keats's work in vain for anything like a statement of what beauty is; but we find everywhere descriptions of what it does. These center around two interrelated ideas: that beauty is life-affirming and that it is consoling. As a result of "being in close relationship with Beauty & Truth," Keats writes to his brothers, "disagreeables evaporate" (*Letters*, 1:192). Beauty exercises an ameliorating effect on human suffering—not a permanent eradication of it but a soothing of the distressed spirit, as Keats suggests near the opening of *Endymion:*

> Spite of despondence, of the inhuman dearth
> Of noble natures, of the gloomy days,
> Of all the unhealthy and o'er-darkened ways
> Made for our searching: yes, in spite of all,
> Some shape of beauty moves away the pall
> From our dark spirits.   (1. 8–13)

In the very next lines Keats lists some examples of beauty:

> Such the sun, the moon,
> Trees old, and young sprouting a shady boon
> For simple sheep; and such are daffodils
> With the green world they live in; and clear rills
> That for themselves a cooling covert make
> 'Gainst the hot season; the mid forest brake,
> Rich with a sprinkling of fair musk-rose blooms:
> And such too is the grandeur of the dooms
> We have imagined for the mighty dead;
> All lovely tales that we have heard or read.
>   (1. 13–22)

The list is not exhaustive, but it suggests three types of beauty that all have a consolatory function: natural, poetic, and religious ("the grandeur of the dooms / We have imagined for the mighty dead"). Three points are crucial here. First, Keats considers religions on the same level as any other beautiful things, and thus characteristically demonstrates his skeptical reduction of all ideologies and his belief that the value of any religion, like any myth or work of art, lies only in its human significance. Second, he reiterates his belief that the central function of poetry is to console men, since beauty "moves away the pall / From our dark spirits." And finally, he implies that poetry shares with religion at least this consolatory function.

Only a few brief examples will suffice here to remind us of how pervasive was Keats's conception of the consolatory function of poetry. Most critics have underestimated its importance for Keats and have failed to see its connection with his conception of poetry's neoreligious role in the modern world.[1] In the early verse epistle "To George Felton Mathew" poets are described as men who try "to flap away each sting / Thrown by the pitiless world" (lines 64–65). The reading of "a debonair / And gentle tale of love and languishment" eases the burden of "One Who Has Been Long in City Pent" (lines 7–8), just as, in "I Stood Tip-toe," a beautiful tale "charms us at once away from all our troubles: / So that we feel uplifted from the world" (lines 138–39). In *The Fall of Hyperion* the poet is "a humanist, Physician to all men" (1. 190); the Grecian urn is "a friend to man" (line 48); and, in a remarkably similar phrase in a letter, Milton is "an active friend to Man" (*Letters*, 1:255).

But poetry or art is only one type of beauty and thus not the only means of consolation. All forms of beauty serve that function. In "Song" ("Stay, ruby-breasted warbler, stay"), written as early as 1814,[2] the poet says of the bird's beautiful melody:

> E'en so the words of love beguile
>   When Pleasure's tree no flower bears,
> And draw a soft endearing smile

> Amid the gloom of grief and tears.
> (lines 21–24)

And in "Keen, Fitful Gusts," the poet does not feel the bite of the symbolically chilling weather and landscape through which he walks, far away from home:

> For I am brimfull of the friendliness
>   That in a little cottage I have found;
> Of fair-hair'd Milton's eloquent distress,
>   And all his love for gentle Lycid drown'd;
> Of lovely Laura in her light green dress,
>   And faithful Petrarch gloriously crown'd.
> (lines 9–14)

He is lifted up and made cheerful by poetry, but also by "friendliness," another type of beauty which is consoling and life-affirming, and which also appears in a new list of beauties later in *Endymion:*

> Thou wast the mountain-top—the sage's pen—
> The poet's harp—the voice of friends—the sun;
> Thou wast the river—thou wast glory won;
> Thou wast my clarion's blast—thou wast my steed—
> My goblet full of wine—my topmost deed:—
> Thou wast the charm of women, lovely Moon!
> (3. 164–69)

Endymion himself acknowledges the mysterious consolatory powers of beauty, figured in terms of the moon:

> What is there in thee, Moon! that thou shouldst move
> My heart so potently? When yet a child
> I oft have dried my tears when thou hast smil'd.
> (3. 142–44)

A few lines later he says:

> In sowing time ne'er would I dibble take,
> Or drop a seed, till thou wast wide awake.
> (3. 153–54)

In addition to consoling man, beauty also enhances life— symbolically in Keats's description here but also quite literally, as Keats suggests near the beginning of the poem when he says of beautiful things: "They alway must be with us, or we die" (1. 33). This suggestion that without beauty there is nothing worth living for must not be associated with a conception of beauty as escape. Beauty, for Keats, is simply that which affirms life. The notion that without beauty there is no reason to live is thus tautological for Keats, since by *beauty* he means precisely that which does make us want to live. It is an extremely radical view but it is perfectly consistent with Keats's extreme skepticism, and it explains his many curious references to poetry as indispensable to life. "I find that I cannot exist without poetry," he tells Reynolds in 1817, "without eternal poetry" (*Letters*, 1:133). Two and a half years later, writing to Haydon about the value of books, he says: "I may say I could not live without them" (*Letters*, 2:220). There is in both of these comments evidence of that unrelenting dedication to poetry which Keats felt throughout his life. But to interpret these statements as indications only of that devotion is seriously to underestimate the extremity of Keats's skepticism and the continual nature of his struggle against despair. As the anguished letters and late poems to Fanny Brawne reveal, the struggle intensified near the end of his life; but it was scarcely confined to that period. "You tell me never to despair," he writes to Haydon as early as 1817; "I wish it was as easy for me to observe the saying—truth is I have a horrid Morbidity of Temperament which has shown itself at intervals—it is I have no doubt the greatest Enemy and stumbling block I have to fear—I may even say that it is likely to be the cause of my disappointment" (*Letters*, 1:142).

This morbidity of temperament does indeed show itself at intervals in Keats's poetry. One need only remember lines like "I have been half in love with easeful Death" or "Now more than ever seems it rich to die" or "Death is Life's high meed"[3] to realize that Keats is never so tendermindedly self-assured in his affirmations as to be securely beyond the threat of despair. "I am in that temper that if I were under Water I would scarcely kick to come to the top," he writes Bailey at one point (*Letters*, 1:287). The fact is that for Keats every affirmation is only a temporary victory. Since he rejects the idea that suffering can be seen as itself a vindication of some kind of divine plan, his affirmations must always be in spite of suffering, and they can never assume the character of insights that reveal some larger justice in which man can forever rest his confidence. If we cannot confidently know why we are on earth, the only issue becomes how we can be happy. And if we can no longer accept the metaphysical certainties of the old formulas for happiness, we must choose to make our own myths, since "every mental pursuit takes its reality and worth from the ardour of the pursuer—being in itself a nothing" (*Letters*, 1:242). "I must take my stand upon some vantage ground and begin to fight," Keats writes; "I must choose between despair & Energy—I choose the latter" (*Letters*, 2:113).

To choose energy is to choose that which dissipates despair and enhances life—which is exactly what beauty does. Since metaphysical truth cannot be certainly known, this human truth, beauty, is really the only truth there is for man, and it must be an intensity of his own making. That is why Keats says, "What the imagination seizes as Beauty must be truth—whether it existed before or not" (*Letters*, 1:184). Lionel Trilling, although he does not develop the point in his essay on Keats's letters, is especially astute about Keats's use of *beauty* and *truth*. Keats "sought strenuously to discover the reason why we should live," Trilling says, "and . . . he called those things good, or beautiful, or true, which induced us to live or which conduced to our health."[4] Truth for Keats is thus usable truth, not metaphysical truth. It is human truth, something satisfying and real by which man can live. As we shall see later, the radical identification of beauty and truth that Keats makes at the end of "Ode on a Grecian Urn" is to be taken quite literally once we understand that he is not referring to metaphysical categories.

Keats's famous conception of Negative Capability is grounded on this same premise:

> several things dovetailed in my mind, & at once it struck me, what quality went to form a Man of Achievement especially in Literature & which Shakespeare possessed so enormously—I mean *Negative Capability*, that is when man is capable of being in uncertainties, Mysteries, doubts, without any irritable reaching after fact & reason—Coleridge, for instance, would let go by a fine isolated verisimilitude caught from the Penetralium of mystery, from being incapable of remaining content with half knowledge. This pursued through Volumes would perhaps take us no further than this, that with a great poet the sense of Beauty overcomes every other consideration, or rather obliterates all consideration.
>
> (*Letters*, 1:193–94)

The reason "Beauty overcomes every other consideration" for a great poet is that the primary object of the real poet is to console man and to reconcile him to life, by revealing and pointing up its concrete beauty. Since metaphysical questions are inevitably surrounded by "uncertainties, Mysteries, [and] doubts," one must be "content with half knowledge" and recognize that the mystery itself, rather than something behind or beyond it, is the true "Penetralium," the true sanctuary, and thus the nutrient milieu of the true poet.

ii

Keats's conception of beauty as the essential human truth and the primary source of consolation should be viewed in the religious context that he himself establishes for it. Time and again in his major poems Keats offers an alternative to traditional religion; in "Ode to Psyche" and "The Eve of St. Agnes" we can begin to see the lineaments of his "recourse somewhat human."

In "Ode to Psyche" Keats declares himself priest of a new goddess:

> Yes, I will be thy priest, and build a fane
> In some untrodden region of my mind,
> Where branched thoughts, new grown with pleasant pain,
> Instead of pines shall murmur in the wind.
>
> (lines 50–53)

But this goddess scarcely resembles Diana in *Endymion*, for Keats realizes that Psyche is a goddess of his own making. "I see, and sing," he says, "by my own eyes inspired" (line 43). In this choice to create a goddess (which I take to be a choice arising out of that same need to choose energy over despair) there is a clear historical consciousness of the modernity of such a procedure. "You must recollect," Keats tells George and Georgiana just before copying out the ode for them in a letter, "that Psyche was not embodied as a goddess before the time of Apulieus the Platonist who lived afteir the Agustan age, and consequently the Goddess was never worshipped or sacrificed to with any of the ancient fervour—and perhaps never thought of in the old religion— I am more orthodox," he adds wryly, "than to let a hethen Goddess be so neglected" (*Letters*, 2:106). Psyche is thus a peculiarly modern goddess, one who is "too late for antique vows, / Too, too late for the fond believing lyre" (lines 36–37) of the old religions, the "happy pieties" (line 41) of "Olympus' faded hierarchy" (line 25). But Psyche is "fairer than these" (line 28), "fairer than Phoebe's sapphire-region'd star" (line 26), the moon that inspired Endymion's fond imaginings. She is fairer because she arises out of and fulfills the need of the human psyche for beauty and meaning. Keats suggests that in "these days so far retir'd / From happy pieties" (lines 40–41), when the fond illusions of the old

35

religions no longer compel belief, one must create one's own gods. Out of a recognition that all gods exist only for man's happiness, one must choose to make life as intense and energetic and vital as possible.

Out of this profound sense that, as Blake put it, "all deities reside in the human breast,"[5] Keats offers to build a "rosy sanctuary" (line 59) for this new goddess, and to dress it

> With the wreath'd trellis of a working brain,
>> With buds, and bells, and stars without a name,
> With all the gardener Fancy e'er could feign,
>> Who breeding flowers, will never breed the same:
> And there shall be for thee all soft delight
>> That shadowy thought can win,
> A bright torch, and a casement ope at night,
>> To let the warm Love in!   (lines 60–67)

Only by a conscious choice to dress the sanctuary with flowers can the gardener Imagination make us see the splendor of this "loveliest vision" (line 24). To choose to build Psyche a rosy sanctuary is to choose energy over despair.

Keats may be claiming to share with Wordsworth a common poetic ground—"the Mind of Man," as Wordsworth put it, "My haunt, and the main region of my song"[6]—but Keats's religious fervor has no reference to anything beyond this world. For Wordsworth it is the marriage of mind and nature that is the cause for celebration and the source of his inspiration. But for Keats, who reverses the whole tradition of the prophet inspired by something beyond him, "I see, and sing, by my own eyes inspired." Keats takes still further the process of religious humanization which he knew Wordsworth had himself advanced.

"Hyperion" and "Ode to Psyche" portray the old religions nostalgically, as "happy pieties" from a vanished age. If

"Written in Disgust of Vulgar Superstition" levels a sharper critique, a rather more bitter condemnation of superstitions that are regarded as "vulgar," "The Eve of St. Agnes" treats the same subject not acidly but ironically, in a sensuously rich mode whose strokes are no less clear for being more gently, lightly applied.

Critics have long recognized the brilliant use Keats makes of contrast in this poem—contrast, as Abrams conveniently summarizes it, between "heat and cold, crimson and silver, youth and age, revelry and austere penance, sensuality and chastity, life and death, hell and heaven."[7] But for our purposes there is one contrast that is more important than all of these, namely, the contrast between the lovers' humanistic affirmation, which Keats looks upon favorably, and both the superstitious brand of Christianity which Madeline earlier embraces and the ascetic kind of Christianity represented unsympathetically in the life-denying, outworn beadsman. "The Eve of St. Agnes" is, in part, a satire on illusions; but it is also, like many of Keats's other major works, a poem which presents a humanistic alternative to the defunct pieties of traditional religion.

As I understand the central critical debate about this poem (which can be conveniently represented by comparing the views of Earl Wasserman with those of Jack Stillinger) the major issue is how we are to interpret the final union of Madeline and Porphyro. Wasserman characteristically regards the poem as a demonstration of Keats's metaphysics, which takes the lovers through a kind of spiritual pilgrimage culminating in a transcendental union that at once validates Keats's conception of the visionary imagination and illuminates his notion of immortality as the repetition of earthly pleasures in a finer tone. Stillinger, on the other hand, considers the poem a powerful demonstration of what he takes to be Keats's later skepticism, which scathingly exposes the illusion of visionary imagination by showing the lovers' alleged spiritual union to be nothing more than the successful conclusion to a vulgar and manipulative seduction of an extremely deceived woman by an extremely cagey man. The main purpose of the poem, Stillinger argues, is, like that of the great odes and "La Belle Dame," to demonstrate that the dreamer turns his back not simply on the pains of life but on life itself, which is of necessity a mixture of joys and sorrows.[8]

One can hardly disagree with Stillinger about Keats's condemnation of the dreamer. There is indeed an important sense in which "The Eve of St. Agnes" belongs with poems like "La Belle Dame" and *The Fall of Hyperion* as an example of Keats's skepticism about the visionary imagination.[9] Yet the dreamer Keats condemns in "The Eve of St. Agnes" is not the Madeline that we find at the end of the poem but the markedly more naive and hoodwinked girl we find participating in vulgar superstition at the beginning. Stillinger assumes that the only alternative to seeing the union of Madeline and Porphyro as naive and empty is to see it as spiritualized beyond mortality, as Wasserman does. Both positions seem to me inaccurate, Wasserman's because it assumes metaphysical intentions which here as elsewhere are foreign to Keats's skepticism, and Stillinger's because it trivializes Madeline's important development in the poem and thus denies Keats the possibility of offering a positive alternative to the deception of dreaming aside from the merely passive acceptance of reality. The positive alternative that Keats presents in the lovers' union constitutes still another version of that fully humanized religion of beauty which emerges not as an escape from reality but as a conscious choice to find consolation in a world of transience and suffering.

The religious language of the poem naturally provides Wasserman with a great deal of his evidence. But if Keats is indeed as skeptical about metaphysics as I have contended; if the "finer tone" letter, for example, is really an argument for achieving whatever happiness we can on earth; and if the imagination is for Keats really a purely human vehicle serving purely human ends—if all of this is true, then we shall find it very difficult to interpret the religious language of the poem in terms of a complex metaphysics involving a serious conception of the visionary imagination and immortality. Nor is it enough to observe that for centuries poets have used religious language in love poetry without any explicitly religious meaning. What we have instead, I think, is a religious imagery whose presence can be discerned in nearly every one of Keats's major poems and letters, and whose function is to establish a traditionally religious context against which Keats can contrast his new religion of beauty.[10]

It is a brilliant technique, and to the extent that it pervades and illuminates Keats's work it reveals how deeply he was affected by and responding to his historical situation. For the tradition of religious belief was still strong in the early nineteenth century, even though it had been coming under increasing attack. Unlike a writer of the early or middle twentieth century, for example, when religious belief has become the exception rather than the rule among the intellectual reading public, Keats could not effectively deal with the issue of spirituality outside the context of traditional religion. Yeats, for example, could construct a system of spirituality out of the "rag-and-bone shop" of his own heart,[11] and express it in the highly individualistic terms of his own mythology; but for Keats it was necessary to express the "holiness of the Heart's affections" (*Letters*, 1:184) in the very terms of the religious tradition which he was therein rejecting.

"St. Agnes' Eve," the poem begins, "Ah, bitter chill it was!"

(line 1). The emphasis on coldness continues throughout the rest of the stanza:

> The owl, for all his feathers, was a-cold;
> The hare limp'd trembling through the frozen grass,
> And silent was the flock in woolly fold:
> Numb were the Beadsman's fingers, while he told
> His rosary, and while his frosted breath,
> Like pious incense from a censer old,
> Seem'd taking flight for heaven, without a death,
> Past the sweet Virgin's picture, while his prayer he saith.
>
> (lines 2–9)

At the end of the poem, "the iced gusts still rave and beat" (line 327), and in the final lines:

> The Beadsman, after thousand aves told,
> For aye unsought for slept among his ashes cold.
>
> (lines 377–78)

Keats is thus careful to frame the poem on both sides with coldness and old age, which suggests an essential view of the world perfectly consistent with his vision of inevitable suffering. He does this, I think, in order to indicate that whatever affirmations occur within the poem must not circumvent this fundamental and unavoidable reality.

Keats shows in the poem four different ways of coming to terms with this reality, and all of them except one are described in religious terms. The exception is the revelers. These are the brutish wassailers whose simplistic response to the problem of suffering and pain is the unrelenting pursuit of pleasure. They drink away the evening in an escape from reality analogous to that which Keats is originally tempted by but ultimately rejects in "Ode to a Nightingale." Emboldened in their hedonistic indulgence, this merciless and "blood-thirsty race" (line 99) would even "murder upon holy days" (line 119). They are the blasphemers, the vulgar desecrators who have no alternative to traditional religion but the merest sensual indulgence. As such, they must be the enemies of Porphyro, who has a higher mission.

The next two options are both versions of traditional religion: the beadsman's asceticism and Madeline's early superstition. So removed is the beadsman from this world that as he walks through the frigid night air with his numb fingers clutching his rosary,

> his frosted breath,
> Like pious incense from a censer old,
> Seem'd taking flight for heaven.
> (lines 6–8)

Even his breath, that most fundamental of all human things, is scarcely of this world. He is an "aged man," and "already had his deathbell rung; / The joys of all his life were said and sung" (lines 21–23). By using the phrase "said and sung," and thus reminding us of the earlier description of the beadsman at his rosary, saying his prayers and perhaps singing his Aves, Keats sharply contrasts the old man's homely and joyless religious life with his past, which presumably did include at least some joys. But now, his joys all passed, and in his old age, the beadsman is the symbolic vehicle for Christianity. Concentrating his energies entirely on some imagined afterlife, he is cut off from the joyful possibilities of this life, and his progress through the poem must be seen as similar to that of the Titans in "Hyperion"—outworn creatures who represent a decaying creed and who eventually, like the beadsman at the end of this poem, sleep among their own cold ashes.

The alternative of Madeline near the beginning of the poem is scarcely more attractive to Keats. At this point Madeline is indeed "hoodwink'd with faery fancy" (line 70); she is deceived because by surrendering herself totally to the "lap of legends old" (line 135), she puts all her trust in a superstition that is based on a sterile conception of love. By contrast with the humanized religion she embraces later, this superstition, for all its apparent charm, is really as life-denying as the beadsman's strict asceticism. Thus there is considerable ambiguity in Keats's description of her as "free from mortal taint" (line 225), for the ironic implication is that it is unfortunate that Madeline is repudiating her mortality by seeking solutions in a legend that denies life and is itself ultimately doomed to extinction, like the beadsman's asceticism.

The messenger of the new religion is Porphyro. There is, to be sure, a certain sportiveness in his attitude towards his prospective affair with Madeline, but it does not seem to me to follow from this that the affair must be regarded as a vulgar or wanton seduction. Lust is not the only alternative to the kind of sex in which the "sweetly shaped" flesh, to use John Crowe Ransom's phrase, is utterly "sublimed away, and furious blood escaped."[12] In fact, what is involved is exactly the same principle of balance between the physical and the spiritual that Keats seems at pains to establish as an ideal in his description of love in *Endymion*. In that poem the Indian Maiden is not merely sensual, but neither is she some bodiless Platonic idealization. The kind of love that can most successfully promote human happiness, Keats suggests, is that which equally eschews both the otherworldly fantasies of an Endymion and the brute physicality of a Circe. The fantasy of the knight in "La Belle Dame" and the debauchery of the revelers in "The Eve of St. Agnes" are equally destructive of human happiness, the former because it promises more than it can deliver, and the latter because it inevitably leads to the sadness of satiety. But when the balance is proper, Keats says in *Endymion*, "Life's self is nourish'd by its proper pith, / And we are nurtured like a pelican brood" (1. 814–15). The right element for life to be nourished on, that is to say, is life itself, not the promise of some fantasy life or afterlife.[13]

This is the assumption on which the elaborate feast of
Madeline and Porphyro is based:

> And still she slept an azure-lidded sleep,
> In blanched linen, smooth, and lavender'd,
> While he from forth the closet brought a heap
> Of candied apple, quince, and plum, and gourd
> With jellies soother than the creamy curd,
> And lucent syrops, tinct with cinnamon;
> Manna and dates, in argosy transferr'd
> From Fez; and spiced dainties, every one,
> From silken Samarcand to cedar'd Lebanon.
>
> (lines 262–70)

One is reminded of the Song of Solomon, the most famous
biblical text of physical love, whose religious overtones
Keats has brilliantly appropriated to his own humanized
religion. The things of this world which, in the Hebraic-
Christian tradition, are sacred only insofar as they are part
of God's creation, become sacred here not because there is
a God but because they are beautiful, which is to say life-
affirming. Such relish in the things of this world, which
Keats also celebrates in "Lines on the Mermaid Tavern" and
which lies somewhere between the *Canterbury Tales* and
Stevens's "Sunday Morning," confers an almost sacramental
character on many of the objects and daily activities of
human life. As he says in the fragmentary "Ode to May"
("Mother of Hermes!"), Keats wants his poetry to be "rich
in the simple worship of a day" (line 14). One is reminded
of Keats's deliciously sensual "beatified Strawberry" (*Letters,*
2:179), and, even more significantly, of the passage in the
"Chamber of Maiden-Thought" letter that describes the
third chamber as "stored with the wine of love—and the
Bread of Friendship" (*Letters,* 1:283). There too the biblical
and sacramental overtones are intentional, not to point to
some otherworldly reality which is the object of our wor-

ship, but to underline the necessity that in a godless world life be "nourish'd by its proper pith," by life itself.

It has been widely observed that, like other elements of the poem, a good deal of the religious imagery that is used to describe the young lovers echoes *Romeo and Juliet.* That is certainly true, and it is also true that there is a long tradition of using religious imagery for secular purposes, especially love. The important point, however, is not *that* Keats uses it but *how* he does.[14]

Even before Madeline makes love with Porphyro and thus symbolically embraces the new humanized religion, Porphyro perceives her from that religious perspective. She is "like a mission'd spirit" (line 193), "like a saint" (line 222) who "seem'd a splendid angel, newly drest, / Save wings, for heaven" (lines 223-24). In the first two of these images the word *like* signals a simile, which conventionally offers a comparison. But at the same time that they suggest a comparison, *like* and *seem'd* also have the force of qualifiers, since Keats is attempting to redefine the very concept of religion on which the comparisons are based. The point is similar to the one Wallace Stevens makes in "Sunday Morning," when he tells us that the sun to which the men chant their devotion is to be understood "not as a god, but as a god might be" (line 94). Like Stevens, Keats is suggesting that his religion is based on human and not transcendent reality, and that is why he is careful to point out that the angel Madeline has no wings.

At this point in the poem, however, Madeline's religion is an escape from life, for she has been told by the old dames that those who give themselves over to this ritual must neither "look behind, nor sideways, but require / Of Heaven with upward eyes for all that they desire" (lines 53-54). As Stillinger points out, "life in the world [for Keats] is an affair in which pleasure and pain are inseparably mixed," and one either accepts this or one "suffers a kind of moral and spiritual emptiness amounting to death."[15]

Though Madeline was indeed hoodwinked, her conversion to Porphyro's humanized religion represents an embracing of life, and I would submit that it represents an embracing of life which does include pain as well as pleasure, sorrow as well as joy. Keats frames his narrative with the stark realities of age, cold, and storm not to suggest that the lovers are oblivious of the darker aspects of life, but to indicate the tragic context in which any human affirmation must occur. Keats is at pains to indicate the momentary character of human consolation, not the naive optimism of hopeful lovers. Therefore, at the very moment of their fulfillment, Keats reminds us that " 'tis dark: the iced gusts still rave and beat" (line 327). By thus contrasting the warmth of the lovers' bed with the bitter cold that surrounds the mansion, Keats can celebrate the lovers' intensity and at the same time reveal the threats which everywhere await it. The technique of contrast, which he employs brilliantly throughout the poem, is thus perfectly suited to express both the inevitability of suffering and the potent possibilities for consolation—however momentary and vulnerable—within that context. The beauty of their love cannot eradicate the stormy world in which they must live; it is against such a world that the lovers build their own, not as an escape but as a means of consolation within it.

It is indeed a spiritual pilgrimage that Porphyro makes to Madeline, and it culminates in an act of passion, of the heightened intensity of life, which makes possible a fusion of the sensuous and the spiritual. "I have the same Idea of all our Passions as of Love," says Keats, "they are all in their sublime, creative of essential Beauty" (*Letters*, 1:184). The union of Madeline and Porphyro is sacred not by reference to some transcendent reality but because it is beautiful,

45

which is to say life-affirming. The three other alternatives to this union are all life-denying: the wassailers because they seek escape from this world, and the beadsman and early Madeline because they put their trust in transcendent reality. Porphyro is right when he tells Madeline he is "no rude infidel" (line 342), for unlike the revelers he has his own kind of religion, even if it is radically different from traditional religion. "Thou art my heaven," he tells her, "and I thine eremite" (line 277). When we remember the ironic implication of the "finer tone" letter, we can better understand what Keats means by "heaven" in this passage and by "paradise" when Madeline's bedroom is earlier described as such (line 244). He does not mean that beauty can make a heaven or a paradise of earth in any permanent way. "I do not at all believe in this sort of perfectibility," Keats tells George and Georgiana just two months after writing "The Eve of St. Agnes"; "the nature of the world will not admit of it" (*Letters*, 2:101). We cannot know if there is an afterlife, but if there is, what happiness there might be in heaven will be like the happiness men know on earth. The wry implication of the "finer tone" letter is that we had therefore better achieve what happiness we can here and now. If Madeline can provide Porphyro with happiness, why not call her a heaven, since heaven, if it exists, would provide a happiness not essentially different from this earthly version?

"Ah, silver shrine," Porphyro says to Madeline,

> here will I take my rest
> After so many hours of toil and quest,
> A famish'd pilgrim,—saved by miracle.
> (lines 337–39)

The miracle is the beauty of love, which, like all beauty, is mysteriously sacred. The luxurious banquet, the images of worship and spiritual pilgrimage, of paradise and heaven, and of the union of Madeline and Porphyro are all meant to suggest this new conception of the sacred, according to which something is sacred because it "bind[s] us to the earth" (*Endymion* 1. 7) and makes us choose energy over despair. I call this a religion of beauty because it is beauty alone, Keats suggests, that can bind us to the earth and make us affirm life.

iii

To the extent that "The Eve of St. Agnes" does not blink human suffering, it is a romance of a curiously non-escapist and characteristically Keatsian sort. For despite Keats's distinction in "Sleep and Poetry" between the poetry of "Flora, and old Pan" (line 102) and that of "the agonies, the strife / Of human hearts" (lines 124–25)—which for convenience I call a distinction between romance or pastoral and tragedy— Keats rarely if ever wrote any pure romance (i.e., poetry from which the awareness of suffering is wholly absent). In these terms, "The Eve of St. Agnes" is a romance framed by tragedy and not a tragedy itself. What is affirmed in this poem is not the beauty that can be found in suffering itself, but the momentary consolation which is possible even within a larger context of suffering. Without denying or seeking permanent escape from suffering, the lovers create, and the poet celebrates, a moment of intensity within that larger context. But Keats is not concerned in this poem to show that one can find in suffering itself some value. That is the business of tragedy, as *King Lear* powerfully demonstrates for Keats:

> the excellence of every Art is its intensity, capable of making all disagreeables evaporate, from their being in close relationship with Beauty & Truth—Examine King Lear & you will find this examplified throughout.
>
> (*Letters*, 1:192)

Tragedy, in other words, can reveal beauty even in suffering.

The affirmation of *King Lear* involves not only a momentary consolation, as in "The Eve of St. Agnes," but the discovery of beauty in the very extremity and depth of human agony.

How can one who insists steadfastly that suffering must neither be evaded nor explained away also insist that suffering can be valuable, indeed beautiful? Surely the brute facts that "women have Cancers" (*Letters*, 1:292), or that young brothers die, cannot in themselves be beautiful. One hesitates to find consistency where there is none, but one also hesitates to attribute inconsistency to a poet who, although not a systematic thinker, elsewhere demonstrates remarkable consistency. What we have here is not a contradiction but a paradox: although suffering must always be seen as a painful inevitability which can lead to a despair against which even beauty offers no easy or permanent remedy, it can still be seen as beautiful.

The paradox is a profound one, and although it can be difficult to understand, it is really a relatively simple idea— simple in the profound way that many of Keats's dazzling insights are simple. Keats tells us that he has "lov'd the principle of beauty in all things" (*Letters*, 2:263). The phrase "in all things" is repeated two other times in the letters, in the "recourse somewhat human" passage when he refers to "the Beautiful. the poetical in all things" (*Letters*, 1:179), and in a letter to his brother and sister-in-law in which he refers to "the mighty abstract Idea I have of Beauty in all things" (*Letters*, 1:403). The key to the paradox is the term *principle*. I think Keats means by "principle of beauty" not that all things are in themselves beautiful but that all things which are not in themselves beautiful can be *made* beautiful by a particular kind of perception.

"As Tradesmen say," Keats writes to Bailey,

> every thing is worth what it will fetch, so probably every mental pursuit takes its reality and worth from the ardour of the pursuer—being in itself a nothing—

Ethereal thing may at least be thus real, divided under three heads—Things real—things semireal—and no things—Things real—such as existences of Sun Moon & Stars and passages of Shakspeare—Things semireal such as Love, the Clouds &c which require a greeting of the Spirit to make them wholly exist—and Nothings which are made Great and dignified by an ardent pursuit—Which by the by stamps the burgundy mark on the bottles of our Minds, insomuch as they are able to "consec[r]ate whate'er they look upon."

(*Letters*, 1:242–43)

It is a strangely metaphysical language Keats uses, but when one scrutinizes it, one quickly realizes that Keats is really not talking metaphysically at all. What he is talking about is beauty, and he has chosen a loaded metaphysical vocabulary in order to explode the very conception of metaphysics and expound an unmetaphysical, indeed antimetaphysical, view. The word *real* occupies a unique and crucial place in Keats's lexicon; particularly in the letters, he usually means by it the same thing he means by *beautiful*, that is, what binds us to the earth, what makes us say yes to life.[16] In a letter to Reynolds, for example, referring to "the pleasure of loving a sister in Law," Keats says: "Things like these, and they are real, have made me resolve to have a care of my health—you must be as careful" (*Letters*, 1:325). At the end of the "Chamber of Maiden-Thought" letter, he uses the word in this same sense:

Tom has spit a leetle blood this afternoon, and that is rather a damper—but I know—the truth is there is something *real* in the World Your third Chamber of Life shall be a lucky and a gentle one—stored with the wine of love—and the Bread of Friendship.

(*Letters*, 1:282–83; emphasis mine)

What Keats calls "Things real—things semireal—and no things" are thus gradations on a scale of the perception of beauty, which require more or less creative activity on the

49

part of the percipient. Some things are beautiful in themselves, such as the sun, the moon, stars, or certain parts of Shakespeare. Other things, like love or clouds, "require a greeting of the Spirit to make them wholly exist"—i.e., an act of imagination to make them beautiful. Still other things "are made Great and dignified by an ardent pursuit" alone, for these "Nothings" are not in themselves beautiful but must be made so.

It is this last category to which suffering belongs. The fact that a woman has cancer or that a young brother dies is of course no more beautiful in itself than are the sufferings and deprivations of King Lear. But the "principle of beauty" exists in *all* things, and thus all things can be made beautiful if they are perceived in the right way. The great demonstration of this principle for Keats is *King Lear,* which is more, not less, beautiful for all its suffering. But not all art can make suffering beautiful, as Benjamin West's painting, "Death on the Pale Horse," vividly dramatizes to Keats as he compares it with *Lear:*

> It is a wonderful picture, when West's age is considered;
> But there is nothing to be intense upon; no women one
> feels mad to kiss; no face swelling into reality. the ex-
> cellence of every Art is its intensity, capable of making
> all disagreeables evaporate, from their being in close
> relationship with Beauty & Truth—Examine King Lear
> & you will find this examplified throughout; but in this
> picture we have unpleasantness without any momentous
> depth of speculation excited, in which to bury its re-
> pulsiveness.   (*Letters,* 1:192)

Most vividly in art but no less importantly in other areas of life, it is the way we perceive things that determines whether or not we can see any value in suffering. But Keats is not unique in believing that. In the "vale of Soul-making" letter, which is his most important explanation of suffering's role in life, he recognizes that all religions have attempted to explain or to justify suffering:

It is pretty generally suspected that the chr[i]stian scheme has been coppied from the ancient persian and greek Philosophers. . . . I think it probable that this System of Soul-making—may have been the Parent of all the more palpable and personal Schemes of Redemption, among the Zoroastrians the Christians and the Hindoos. For as one part of the human species must have their carved Jupiter; so another part must have the palpable and named Mediatior and saviour, their Christ their Oromanes and their Vishnu.

(*Letters*, 2:103)

If one views the world from a Judaic perspective, for example, suffering will be considered an indication of an inscrutably divine justice, as it is in the Book of Job. The Christian, likewise, will interpret suffering according to the doctrine of *felix culpa*, by which the prospect of salvation renders any suffering just. But if, like Keats, one thinks that placing faith in any kind of higher reality must always be dangerously deceptive, then suffering will be viewed only in a human context. Its rewards, if any, must be experienced in this life. Only in this kind of fully human framework can suffering be seen as beautiful.

The "vale of Soul-making" letter, then, presents a "grander system of salvation than the chryst⟨e⟩ain religion" (*Letters*, 2:102). And it is grander precisely because, by locating salvation in this world rather than in some afterworld, it is more *real*, in the Keatsian sense of beautiful or life-affirming.[17] But there is no suggestion that there is some kind of essential or intrinsic rightness or justice that characterizes all aspects of life and therefore includes suffering. What Keats suggests, instead, is that to fully actualize the soul, or potential identity with which each person is born, one must not merely passively tolerate suffering but actively confront it, as the Indian Maid does in *Endymion:*

Come then, Sorrow!
Sweetest Sorrow!

Like an own babe I nurse thee on my breast.

(4. 279–81)

This does not mean that one must seek suffering or that, like Rimbaud, one must search out the most intense and various experiences in order to savor even the gruesome and perverse for their full cargo of "life." For Keats suffering was not a rare commodity; no one need fear he would be denied his fair share.

Nonetheless, the idea of intensity is of the first importance for Keats's resolution of the problems posed by both suffering and skepticism, since it is only through intense perception or experience that human reality becomes spiritualized. Just as, according to Keats's conception of Negative Capability, the intense perception of beauty allows one to remain content with, and even relish, "uncertainties, Mysteries, [and] doubts," so the intense experience of suffering ironically helps one to bear that suffering and even to deepen one's attachment to life. A comment by William Hazlitt, who influenced Keats profoundly, can illuminate the point if we remember that for Keats beauty is that which is life-affirming. "The keenness of immediate suffering," says Hazlitt in his lecture "On Poetry in General," "*makes us drink deeper of the cup of human life;* tugs at the heartstrings; loosens the pressure about them; and calls the springs of thought and feeling into play with tenfold force."[18] For Keats the intense experience of suffering somehow makes us cherish life all the more, just as a dying man who may feel great sorrow in leaving the world may also feel a new tenderness for it. One must open oneself so fully to one's experience that even suffering—without being blinked or transcended—will be seen to have some value:

> I will call the *world* a School instituted for the purpose of teaching little children to read—I will call the *human heart* the *horn Book* used in that School—and I will call the *Child able to read, the Soul* made from that

school and its *hornbook*. Do you not see how necessary
a World of Pains and troubles is to school an Intelligence and make it a soul? A Place where the heart must
feel and suffer in a thousand diverse ways!

(*Letters,* 2:102)

Soul-making is thus the process by which one develops
one's identity; to school one's intelligence and make it a soul
is to humanize it. But what is the value of soul-making? It
seems to me of the utmost significance that Keats never
argues that it is valuable, but only suggests that it is by employing a loaded religious vocabulary, whose assumptions
he can then deftly and subtly undermine. If souls are desirable for Keats, they are not so by reference to the higher
realities of traditional religion. After all, his is a humanized
system of salvation set in direct opposition to the "little cir-
cumscribe[d] straightened notion" of Christianity, which is
based on the "arbit[r]ary interposition of God" (*Letters,* 2:
102). Nor can Keats's references to God, which have something like the status of Wordsworth's myth of pre-existence
in the "Immortality" ode, nullify the radically untraditional
assumption that souls are not divinely but humanly created,
that people are not born with souls but must themselves
make them, and in the process move beyond the immature
status of "I[n]telligences," which "in short . . . are God"
(*Letters,* 2:102). They must do so not through the intervention of some mediator of a higher reality but through living
intensely in this world. Whether or not God exists cannot be
definitely known, but if he does, the business of man involves a development away from him, just as, if immortality
exists, the business of man is to achieve what happiness he
can in *this* world.

By thus employing religious terminology to describe
what amounts to a process of humanization (notice, in addition, that he calls the human heart "the Minds Bible"
[*Letters,* 2:103]), Keats can attach a neoreligious signifi-

cance to what in fact is extreme secularization. A soul, which is the product of this process of humanization, becomes, in this new religious sense, one more variety of beauty, and like most other beautiful things, it is an intensity of one's own making. The "principle of beauty" may exist "in all things," even suffering, but only by seeing life in a totally humanized perspective—and experiencing it intensely, including its sorrows—can one see it as beautiful. If there is any value in schooling an intelligence into a soul, it is the same value that attaches to any other kind of beauty: it binds us to the earth; it makes us say yes to life.

$$iv$$

Keats's new humanized religion was justified on purely pragmatic rather than metaphysical grounds. What mattered most was that beauty really was life-affirming, and could thus provide a source of affirmation and consolation which avoided the "pious frauds of Religion" (*Letters*, 2:80). Human life itself, if seen properly, had within it the basis of its own affirmation, a principle of beauty that could be disclosed the more, not the less, readily as one confronted its totality rather than avoiding its darker side. In Keats's most fully realized lyrics, life is perceived as beautiful by being viewed in its bittersweet totality—a completeness that is beautiful in the most humanized terms, according to which transience and death are miseries indeed, but also beautiful.

A tentative, perhaps overly generalized treatment of this theme occurs in the sonnet "Four Seasons Fill the Measure of the Year":

> Four seasons fill the measure of the year;
>> There are four seasons in the mind of man:
> He has his lusty Spring, when fancy clear
>> Takes in all beauty with an easy span:

He has his Summer, when luxuriously
   Spring's honied cud of youthful thought he loves
To ruminate, and by such dreaming nigh
   His nearest unto heaven: quiet coves
His soul has in its Autumn, when his wings
   He furleth close; contented so to look
On mists in idleness—to let fair things
   Pass by unheeded as a threshold brook.
He has his Winter too of pale misfeature,
Or else he would forego his mortal nature.

Keats copies this sonnet in a letter to Bailey immediately after the passage about real, semireal, and no things, which ends with Keats's claim that our minds have the capacity— and here he misquotes Shelley—"to 'consec[r]ate *whate'er they look upon*[.]' I have written," he says, "a Sonnet here of a somewhat collateral nature" (*Letters*, 1:243). All things, the poem suggests, can be seen as beautiful, even "no things" like the suffering symbolized by winter. These can be made beautiful "by an ardent pursuit," which here involves seeing suffering and transience within the larger context not of some higher reality but of the cycle and rhythm of human life. If autumn, like spring, "hast [its] music too" ("To Autumn," line 24), so does summer and even winter. For man to "forego his mortal nature," which includes transience, suffering, and death, denies him the life-giving if paradoxical perception that the principle of beauty is in *all* things, even suffering. Keats masterfully expresses the same paradox in "Hyperion," where he describes Thea staring at Saturn, who is asleep and has not yet learned of the imminent destruction of his race of Titans. "How beautiful," Keats says, "if sorrow had not made / Sorrow more beautiful than Beauty's self" (1. 35–36).

It is worth remembering in this connection Keats's ultimate reservations about the "Cold Pastoral" (line 45) of the Grecian urn as he compares it with the warm and sentient reality of the human. The fantasy of escape into a timeless

world beyond the weakness of the flesh is severely chal-
lenged in that poem, while in "Ode to a Nightingale" the
imagined realm of total fulfillment turns out to be nothing
other than death. For all its vulnerability to suffering, and
for all its inevitable contamination by the constrictions and
ravages of time, the transient, mortal condition must itself
be the source of any affirmation.

It is precisely this condition that Keats celebrates in the
"Bright Star" sonnet. The kind of steadfastness that Keats
is drawn to in the star lies not in the "lone splendour" of its
otherworldliness but in the desire for an erotic passion that
in its "unchangeable[ness]" would "live ever" (lines 2, 9, 14).
It is precisely because that moment of supreme intensity
cannot be preserved that Keats longs to preserve it and
cherishes it, here as in "Ode on a Grecian Urn" and "To
Autumn." Like those and many of his other poems, "Bright
Star" is concerned with the human response to change, and
the magnificent tidal image of "the moving waters at their
priestlike task / Of pure ablution round earth's human
shores" (lines 5–6) suggests that there is a kind of holiness
in the very process of change. It is a holiness which, along
with most other forms of holiness, Matthew Arnold felt,
only thirty years later in "Dover Beach," had disappeared
from the world:

> The Sea of Faith
> Was once, too, at the full, and *round earth's shore*
> Lay like the folds of a bright girdle furl'd.
> But now I only hear
> Its melancholy, long, withdrawing roar.
>   (lines 21–25; emphasis mine)

"To Autumn," which I take to be Keats's purest celebration of the transient mortal condition, involves a sanctifica-
tion of the human that goes quite beyond mere resignation
or passive acceptance. Sunset, night, and winter hover along
the poem's periphery, but the foreshadowing of death, far

from haunting or escaping the poem's affirmation, gives it its inclusive character. The poet is totally undisturbed by the recurrent foreshadowing and subtly resonating imminence of death. For at this supremely luxurious moment of fruition he is able to view the external world of nature from the point of view of one who fully accepts his mortality and recognizes that nature will survive him. Only by living intensely in the present moment can one discover that autumn has its own music.

Keats can hear that poignant music only because he views the natural world in human terms. The personification of Autumn is so completely humanized that the poet actually consoles the season: "Where are the songs of Spring? Ay, where are they? / Think not of them, thou hast thy music too" (lines 23–24). The fact that these lines could easily refer to Keats's consoling himself only reinforces the humanization. For Keats personifies Autumn in order to suggest that, although nature may survive all our interpretations of it, its value or, in Keats's sense of the word, its "truth" lies only in its human significance. "Scenery is fine," he tells Bailey, "but human nature is finer—The Sward is richer for the tread of a real, nervous, english foot—the eagles nest is finer for the Mountaineer has look'd into it" (*Letters*, 1:242).[19] Like religion, nature's significance for Keats lies in its capacity to enhance human life. The over-ripeness and plentiful bounty of nature in this poem are meant to express the rich and magnificent fullness of life. But life can only be seen in this way when it is viewed from a human perspective. Keats's "lambs [that] loud bleat from hilly bourn" (line 30) derive their sacramental character not from a divine reality that transcends this world, as Blake's famous lamb does, but from a reality that is spiritualized by intense human perception of it. It is in this same humanized sense that Autumn combines with the sun to "bless / With fruit the vines" (lines 3–4). The most profound beauty can be disclosed only to those who recognize, in Wallace Stevens's phrase, that "Death is the mother of beauty,"[20] and it is because Keats has such a recognition that he can accept, with consummate intensity and "disinterestedness" (*Letters*, 2:79), the fragile equilibrium in which beauty and transience are poised in this world.

Wordsworth has a similar recognition at the end of the "Immortality" ode:

> The clouds that gather round the setting sun
> Do take a sober coloring from an eye
> That hath kept watch o'er man's mortality;
> Another race hath been, and other palms are won.
> Thanks to the human heart by which we live,
> Thanks to its tenderness, its joys, and fears,
> To me the meanest flower that blows can give
> Thoughts that do often lie too deep for tears.
> (lines 198–205)

Like Keats, the more he feels his mortality, the more vital and fresh and precious the things of this world seem. "How astonishingly," says Keats a year before his death, "does the chance of leaving the world impress a sense of its natural beauties on us. Like poor Falstaff, though I do not babble, I think of green fields. I muse with the greatest affection on every flower I have known from my infancy . . . I have seen foreign flowers in hothouses of the most beautiful nature, but I do not care a straw for them. The simple flowers of our sp[r]ing are what I want to see again" (*Letters*, 2:260). Those simple flowers may resemble Wordsworth's "meanest flower that blows" but there is this important difference: for Keats it is the flowers in and of themselves that matter, rather than their participation in the grand union of mind and nature. The actual flowers are beautiful. That is enough.

In "Ode on Melancholy" Keats explores the way in which

this same curiously symbiotic relationship between beauty and transience inevitably involves melancholy. In the opening lines, he rejects suicide as a proper response to the "anguish of the soul" (line 10):

> No, no, go not to Lethe, neither twist
>   Wolf's-bane, tight-rooted, for its poisonous wine;
> Nor suffer thy pale forehead to be kiss'd
>   By nightshade, ruby grape of Proserpine;
> Make not your rosary of yew-berries,
>   Nor let the beetle, nor the death-moth be
>   Your mournful Psyche, nor the downy owl
> A partner in your sorrow's mysteries.
>
> (lines 1–8)

The images of death and poisoning are so explicit here that one wonders why so many critics have softened the urgency of this stanza by reading it, as Miriam Allott does, as a statement that "true Melancholy is not to be found among thoughts of oblivion, death and gloom."[21] Wolfsbane and nightshade do not simply distract you from true melancholy; they kill you. As Allott herself indicates, Keats had recently been reading that section of Burton's *The Anatomy of Melancholy* which deals specifically with the kind of "melancholy that leads to suicide," and Keats's "ode is in effect a reply."[22] The question of where one can find melancholy becomes crucial in the poem but at the beginning the pressing question is how to respond to it.

Instead of seeking oblivion, Keats suggests in the second stanza, one should seek the healing powers of beauty:

> But when the melancholy fit shall fall
>   Sudden from heaven like a weeping cloud,
> That fosters the droop-headed flowers all,
>   And hides the green hill in an April shroud;
> Then glut thy sorrow on a morning rose,
>   Or on the rainbow of the salt sand-wave,
>   Or on the wealth of globed peonies.
>
> (lines 11–17)

Keats insists here on the ability of beautiful things—natural things of this world—to make us embrace life even in our sorrow. The prerequisite, as always, is intensity:

> Or if thy mistress some rich anger shows,
>   Emprison her soft hand, and let her rave,
>   And feed deep, deep upon her peerless eyes.
>   (lines 18–20)

In the third stanza Keats turns this idea on its head. If beauty consoles us in our melancholy, it is also true that the very delights of beauty must soon yield again to melancholy. The rose and the peonies will wither, and the exquisite rainbow cast over the sea-water in the sand-wave will fade. There is "grief," as Cynthia says in *Endymion,* "in the very deeps of pleasure" (2. 823–24). The beauty that consoles us is "Beauty that must die" (line 21), for nothing can ever permanently eradicate the melancholy of human existence. It needs to be reemphasized that Keats's aestheticism, his solution to the problems posed by his skepticism and the inevitability of suffering, has the character of temporary consolation rather than apocalyptic transfiguration. Keats refuses to gloss over the fact that melancholy "dwells with Beauty" (line 21) and with

> Joy, whose hand is ever at his lips
>   Bidding adieu; and aching Pleasure nigh,
>   Turning to Poison while the bee-mouth sips.
>   (lines 22–24)

In such a world, as we have already seen in "The Eve of St. Agnes," fleeting moments of joy must be cherished and celebrated.

But moments of joy, free from sorrow, are not our only consolation:

> Ay, in the very temple of Delight
>   Veil'd Melancholy has her sovran shrine,
>   Though seen of none save him whose strenous tongue

Can burst Joy's grape against his palate fine.

(lines 25–28)

No one, Keats says, can see Melancholy's shrine except those who live with intensity and perceive with intensity. What those people will discover is not only that Melancholy has a shrine but that it is located "in the very temple of Delight." Now there is a pregnant ambiguity here, which is related to the symbiotic relationship between beauty and joy on the one hand and transience and melancholy on the other. It is sad, on the one hand, that even in "the very temple of Delight" there is Melancholy. It is sad that beauty is ephemeral. But Keats is also telling us another truth: that it is the fact of transience that makes beauty meaningful, and that, if properly perceived, melancholy itself can be seen as beautiful, for it has its shrine not in the temple of despair but of delight. Although sorrow is considered inescapable, it is also regarded as a prerequisite for the most consoling beauty, just as in the "vale of Soul-making" letter suffering is both inevitable and necessary to the development of the soul: "Do you not see how necessary a World of Pains and troubles is to school an Intelligence and make it a soul? A Place where the heart must feel and suffer in a thousand diverse ways!" (*Letters*, 2:102).

In my discussion of that letter, I said that the soul is implicitly considered another form of beauty, and that like most other forms of beauty, it must be created by intensity of perception and experience. Keats seems to be making exactly these points about melancholy in this ode: that it should be seen as a kind of beauty and that it can only become beautiful if we experience it intensely. The image of melancholy as a rainfall that revives the drooping flowers suggests those life-giving qualities of beauty that Keats links with joy in the image of the grape. To release joy's potent juices one must burst its grape, though doing so will paradoxically destroy it. Sorrow and joy cannot be separated.

As he says in "Welcome Joy, and Welcome Sorrow," "I do love you both together!" (line 4).

In my discussion of the "vale of Soul-making" letter I also said that by setting up a religious context—by alluding to other religions and using loaded religious language—Keats not only attaches a value to soul-making which he never specifically argues, but he thereby elevates the value to a religious status. In "Ode on Melancholy" he employs exactly this procedure in order to establish that if we do properly perceive melancholy, it discloses a religious value of a new kind.

Keats has taken great pains in this poem to construct an elaborate religious context in which he can locate his own view. There are, first of all, the allusions to Greek mythology: to Lethe, Proserpine, and Psyche, and, in the final line, to the Greek and Roman practice of putting trophies in the gods' temples. Then there is the allusion to Christianity, the "rosary" of line 5. There is also the "beetle" of line 6, which, Abrams tells us, "refers to replicas of the . . . scarab, which were often placed by Egyptians in their tombs as a symbol of resurrection." Finally, there are the more general religious references: the "heaven" of line 12; the "mysteries" of line 8, which Abrams glosses as "secret religious rites";[23] the two references to the "soul" (lines 10, 29); and the personification of Melancholy as a goddess who has a "shrine" (line 26) in a "temple" (line 25). One finds it hard to imagine that Keats would employ so many religious trappings merely for embellishment. The more plausible explanation, which is supported by his use of religious contexts in almost all of his major poems and letters, is that the religious issue is central to the poem. But the poem itself is the best proof of that.

Just as, in the "vale of Soul-making" letter, Keats describes the process of humanization as soul-making and thus attaches religious significance to it, so in this poem he attaches religious significance to melancholy by personifying it as a goddess and giving it a temple and a shrine. Those who can see the shrine are those who embrace human life, including its painful aspects, and they are contrasted with those others in the first stanza who respond to melancholy by seeking escape from it. Structurally, Keats embodies this contrast by devoting the first stanza to the latter and the second to the former. He heightens the contrast by emphasizing death and some realm beyond the mortal world in the first stanza, and life and the natural world in the second.[24] The first stanza is crowded with religious allusions, while in the second stanza there is only one, in the image of the "melancholy fit" falling "sudden from heaven" (lines 11-12). But is it not an unusual heaven that dispenses fits of melancholy to men? Clearly it is no Christian heaven. In fact, as we have seen, melancholy springs directly out of joy, so that Keats seems to be using "heaven" here in the same sense that Porphyro did when he called Madeline his heaven: the source of joy. But if heaven is the source of both melancholy and delight, it must be identical with beauty, since that, Keats tells us in the poem, is the source of them both. If beauty, as the second stanza makes clear, is located in this and not some other world, then heaven too must be located on earth.

Keats's humanization of heaven—bringing it down to earth and suggesting that it is the source of melancholy as well as joy—is consistent with the poem's argument that the world is imperfect, that melancholy can never be banished from human experience. But it is also consistent with the other side of that argument—that melancholy itself can be seen as beautiful, and that as such it has a new religious significance: it binds us to the earth. By embracing this world in an attitude of "wakeful anguish," one's "soul shall taste the sadness of [Melancholy's] might" (lines 10, 29)—of her power, I take it, for soul-making, for the creation of beauty.

But the discovery of beauty in melancholy has a rather special value in this poem, since it offers a basis on which one can reject suicide and affirm life without in any way evading or explaining away its anguish. And that is why it is preferable to all the other religions alluded to in the poem. The Greeks must have recourse to a myth of an afterlife of forgetfulness, the Egyptians must have their symbols of resurrection, and the Christians must have their rosaries and their conception of a heaven of perfect bliss. All of these religions posit a world beyond the one we know on earth in order to console man for the sorrows of life. But Keats's new religion offers an explanation of suffering that is based only on human truth, and if it is all we know on earth, to borrow the terminology of "Ode on a Grecian Urn," it is also all we need to know.

The notion that suffering is absolutely necessary to the process of soul-making, or developing one's individual humanity, can be clarified by considering the words of the modern Spanish writer Miguel de Unamuno. While Unamuno is ultimately at pains in *The Tragic Sense of Life* to prove that suffering confirms the existence of God, his comments are otherwise astonishingly Keatsian. "He who does not suffer," says Unamuno:

> and who does not suffer because he does not live, is that . . . impassive entity, which because of its impassivity is nothing but a pure idea. . . . But the world suffers, and suffering is the sense of the flesh of reality; it is the spirit's sense of its mass and substance; it is the self's sense of its own tangibility; it is immediate reality.
>
> Suffering is the substance of life and the root of personality, for it is only suffering that makes us persons. . . . Suffering is a spiritual thing. It is the most immediate revelation of consciousness. . . . A man who

had never known suffering, either in greater or less degree, would scarcely possess consciousness of himself.[25]

The assumption that underlies the "vale of Soul-making" letter and "Ode on Melancholy," and that makes their discovery of value in suffering and melancholy a paradox rather than a contradiction, is in some ways tragic. It shares with tragedy the belief that human beings can never know the secrets of destiny, can never fully penetrate the mystery of the universe, and that to fully actualize one's human nature is inevitably to suffer. But the tragedian nonetheless finds beauty in the totally realized human life, even if it does always exhibit the disastrous flaw of blindness to fate. There is beauty in the life of a Beowulf or an Oedipus, a dignity, a grandeur stemming from a sense of completion and intensity. As Keats's example of *King Lear* suggests, suffering can be viewed as beautiful at the same time that it is seen as suffering, in literature as in life. Tragedy, in fact, is for Keats the most consoling kind of literature because it evades nothing yet shows life's possibilities of beauty all the same.

But suffering can be overplayed, in life as well as in literature, and in his verse epistle "To J. H. Reynolds Esq." Keats urges a principle of balance. "I was at home," he writes:

> And should have been most happy—but I saw
> Too far into the sea; where every maw
> The greater on the less feeds evermore:—
> But I saw too distinct into the core
> Of an eternal fierce destruction,
> And so from Happiness I far was gone.
> Still am I sick of it: and though to-day
> I've gathered young spring-leaves, and flowers gay
> Of Periwinkle and wild strawberry,
> Still do I that most fierce destruction see.
>
> (lines 92–102)

To dwell exclusively on the dark side of life, to see life as irredeemably cruel, miserable, and meaningless, is inevitably to make one's own life miserable and meaningless. That is why Keats offers a prayer in "Lines Written in the Highlands," "that man may never lose his mind on mountains bleak and bare" (lines 45–46). But at the other extreme is an equally certain guarantor of unhappiness, the aspiration to ideals that cannot be attained and can never endure. This is the illusion of an Endymion, of one whose "imagination," in the words of the epistle to Reynolds, has been

> brought
> Beyond its proper bound, yet still confined,—
> Lost in a sort of Purgatory blind.   (lines 78–80)

Keats makes the point directly:

> It is a flaw
> In happiness to see beyond our bourn—
> It forces us in summer skies to mourn:
> It spoils the singing of the Nightingale.
>   (lines 82–85)

This is exactly what happens to Endymion and to anyone, Keats suggests, who bases his hopes for happiness on impossible ideals.

Rather than imposing our desires on the world in this illusory and inevitably frustrating manner, we ought to take our cues from the actual world itself:

> O that our dreamings all of sleep or wake
> Would all their colours from the Sunset take:
> From something of material sublime,
> Rather than shadow our own Soul's daytime
> In the dark void of Night.   (lines 67–71)

The simple image of the sunset is masterful, for it suggests that combination of earthly and spiritual, also described by "material sublime," that Keats is attempting to establish as the ideal of human aspiration. The image of sunset also expresses that conjunction of transience and beauty which is at the foundation of Keats's affirmation of life and his program for poetry.

The synthesis Keats seeks applies both to life and to art. The best poetry will reflect a view of life that promotes human happiness, and such a view requires that one be aware not only of the beautiful in life but also of the impermanence of beauty. The tragic context of beauty cannot be evaded. The sunset may be beautiful, but part of its beauty stems from our awareness that it will soon be replaced by darkness. But we must also remember, as Keats says in "To Homer," that "on the shores of darkness there is light" (line 9). In poetry as in life, the beauty that will truly promote human happiness is beauty in its terrestrial context, which is defined by transience.

Keats's ideals for life were intimately related to his ideals for poetry. Although he never avoided suffering in his poems, neither did he very often allow himself to remain transfixed, staring "into the core / Of an eternal fierce destruction," without seeing something of the beauty which even the darkest aspects of human life could disclose. Suffering and skepticism may be the bedrock on which Keats erects his poetic edifice, but his own poetry testifies to his belief that poetry itself must be beautiful in its own texture and design, and that it must provide a vision of the world which, in the absence of traditional religion, promotes the possibilities of genuine human happiness.

III

The Program for Poetry

As a solution to the problems posed by skepticism and as a remedy against the sting of suffering, aestheticism was for Keats a principle of life, which was not restricted to but emphatically embraced poetry or art. Poetry for Keats, although it had some unique advantages of its own (its permanence, for example, and its ability to make us aware of beauty), was only one among many forms of beauty, and as such it shared both the limitations and the possibilities of other types of beauty. It is extremely important that we realize Keats viewed poetry in this way, because it explains both his critique of the kind of poetry that makes dangerously unrealistic claims and his own peculiarly high claims for poetry of a totally humanized kind. Keats understood very early that poetry must perform exactly the same consolatory and life-affirming function that all other beauty performs. He knew that the real challenge of writing original poetry was to do so without the traditional religious support and metaphysical certainty on which most of the great poetry of the past had been grounded, including that of the first generation of romantics. Poetry must answer the same need that all other types of beauty do: the need to find some means of endurance and affirmation in a painful world devoid of the old gods. In answering that need poetry must assume the traditional religious function of consolation, and in administering that charge, in serving, as Keats says in *The Fall of Hyperion*, as "a humanist, Physician to all men" (1. 190), the poet must take upon himself the neo-religious task of adding "a mite to that mass of beauty which is harvested . . . by the finest spirits, and put into etherial existence for the relish of one's fellows" (*Letters*, 1:301).

———

Keats's conception of the religious nature of poetry can even be seen in some of his more fanciful or lighthearted poems. In "Ode to Apollo" ("God of the golden bow"), for example, Keats playfully chides himself for having trivialized the significance of Apollo by joining Leigh Hunt in wearing a laurel crown. The tone is half-mocking as Keats declares his guilt and begs for absolution for his sin of blasphemy:

> The Pleiades were up.
>   Watching the silent air;
> The seeds and roots in Earth
>   Were swelling for summer fare;
>   The Ocean, its neighbour,
>   Was at his old labour,
>   When, who—who did dare
> To tie for a moment thy plant round his brow,
>   And grin and look proudly,
>   And blaspheme so loudly,
> And live for that honour, to stoop to thee now?
>   O Delphic Apollo!
>   (lines 25–36)

Despite the obvious humor and the relatively frivolous tone, there is an underlying sense of sincerity in this poem, and it seems fair to say that Keats's self-reproach does have a connection with his serious conception of the new religious mission of poetry.

"'Tis the 'witching time of Night'" is considerably more serious. The poem is full of the trappings of a lullaby for the Christ child: the cradle, the swath, the lambs, the repetition of "child," the simple, innocent language, and the prophetic tone. However, it prophesies not a religious saviour but a poet:

> Amaze, amaze!
> It stares, it stares, it stares,
> It dares what no one dares!
> It lifts its little hand into the flame
> Unharm'd, and on the strings
> Paddles a little tune, and sings,
> With dumb endeavor sweetly—
> Bard art thou completely!
> > Little child
> > O' th' western wild,
> Bard art thou completely!
> Sweetly with dumb endeavor
> A Poet now or never,
> > Little child
> > O' th' western wild,
> A Poet now or never!
>
> (lines 41–56)

The poem was written for Keats's brother and sister-in-law and their child in America; but in its prophetic fervor, its conscious appropriation of a traditional religious context for new religious purposes, and its brilliant exploitation of the myth of the new world, it is still another version, however distinct in tone and emphasis, of the essential theme of "Written in Disgust of Vulgar Superstition."

One cannot emphasize enough how pervasive is Keats's conviction that poetry must now assume the consolatory function of religion. Most critics, as I have already suggested, have considered consolation merely a minor aspect of Keats's conception of the function of poetry. Morris Dickstein, for example, whose view is not untypical if a bit extreme, asserts that the "notion of art as therapy or consolation" is something that Keats "unconvincingly offered in 'Sleep and Poetry.'" He admits that the proem of *Endymion* "professes a subtler version" of art as consolation, and though he even acknowledges the similarity in conception of the famous disputed lines of *The Fall of Hyperion*, he argues that Keats's very disenchantment with the idea was

70

what caused him to delete those lines.[1] Not only does Dickstein's argument strike me as a curiously evasive way of dealing with this and quite a bit of other evidence, but it also reveals an attitude of condescension towards Keats's poetry, especially his early poetry, which I find as widespread as it is unwarranted and misleading.

No one can dispute the inferiority of Keats's early verse in comparison with his mature work. But formal weakness or technical imperfection need not imply conceptual confusion or uncertainty. In Keats, in fact, I think we have an extraordinary example of a poet whose essential ideas about life and poetry were almost fully conceived from the beginning of his poetic career, despite his constant revaluation of them. By ignoring Keats's effort to attribute a new religious function to poetry, a critic like Dickstein misconstrues Keats's conception of the consolatory function of poetry, incorrectly assuming Keats means by it a process which offers "at least the illusion of an escape" from life's difficulties.[2] When he puts it in these terms, Dickstein is quite right to deny the notion any significance. But once we realize that Keats intentionally establishes a religious context for the function of poetry in "Sleep and Poetry," *Endymion*, the two "Hyperion" poems, "Ode on a Grecian Urn," and numerous other poems and letters, it becomes clear that the consolatory conception of poetry suggested in them is perfectly consistent with the rest of Keats's humanized religion of beauty.[3]

ii

In "Sleep and Poetry" we find the first extended expression of Keats's dedication to poetry. Even more importantly, he presents his reasons and justification for the dedication, along with an outline of his poetic program and career. There has been a great deal of confusion about the significance of the poem's title. It has been suggested, by Bate for example, that the poem's major interest is in the relationship between revery and poetry; or by Aileen Ward that

> sleep and poetry, the rather odd set of contrasts on which he built his poem, were . . . not an antithesis but a necessary ebb and flow of poetic power. . . . Time after time the poet must surrender to the health-giving delights of the body, give rein to its hungers and draw new strength from their satisfactions in order to rise again to the discipline of art.[4]

But the central relationship between sleep and poetry that Keats is at pains to express here is considerably less complicated than all this. It is mainly an analogy that he is drawing: poetry refreshes us and gives new strength to our spirits, just as sleep does to our bodies.

Sleep is variously described in the first stanza as "gentle," "soothing," "tranquil," "healthful," "secret," "serene," and "full of visions." It is, that is to say, a restorative, enabling us to awake each day refreshed. "The morning blesses / Thee," Keats says to Sleep in the following lines, "for enlivening all the cheerful eyes / That glance so brightly at the new sun-rise" (lines 16–18). It comes as a surprise, then, to discover at the end of the poem that the poet arises refreshed even though he has *not* slept:

> the morning light
> Surprised me even from a sleepless night;
> And up I rose refresh'd, and glad, and gay.
> (lines 399–401)

How can he arise refreshed without sleeping? Because he has spent the night with poetry. Like sleep, poetry has performed its symbolic function of restoration, consistent with "the great end / Of Poesy," which, as Keats tells us in the poem, is to "be a friend / To sooth the cares, and lift the thoughts of man" (lines 246–47). He has spent the night contemplating poetry and as a result his strength has been renewed. It is an ingenious method Keats has devised to support the consolatory, life-enhancing conception of poetry which the rest of the poem argues, for by making poetry analogous to a naturally and vitally human function, he both suggests the broadly humanistic context in which he views poetry and underlines its importance.

That poetry now replaces religion as a vital and significant means of consolation is emphasized by Keats in the extravagantly elaborate religious imagery which pervades the poem. Poetry is first described as "awful" and "holy," "chacing away all worldliness and folly," and even (in an image of the Old Testament Jehovah) "coming sometimes like fearful claps of thunder" (lines 25–27). At other times it makes us exclaim, "Rejoice! rejoice!" (line 38). The long address to "Poesy," which begins at line 47, is couched almost entirely in religious terms. Reference is made to the poet's "ardent prayer" at "thy sanctuary"; to the "mountain-top" where the poet will "kneel . . . until I feel / A glowing splendour"; twice to the "wide heaven" of poesy; and finally to "a fresh sacrifice" and "an eternal book" of nature (lines 47–64). Keats's attack on eighteenth-century poetry refers to the whole enterprise as a "schism" (line 181) whose perpetrators were an "impious race! / That blasphemed" Apollo (lines 201–2). And his address to the Muses is filled with religious imagery as well:

> Whose congregated majesty so fills
> My boundly reverence, that I cannot trace
> Your hallowed names, in this unholy place.
> (lines 208–10)

But the most significant religious imagery of all is that which describes how clearly Keats has seen his "vast idea":

> there ever rolls
> A vast idea before me, and I glean
> Therefrom my liberty; thence too I've seen
> The end and aim of Poesy. 'Tis clear
> As any thing most true; as that the year

73

> Is made of the four seasons—manifest
> As a large cross, some old cathedral's crest.
>   (lines 290–96)

The vast idea is the "principle of beauty in all things" or, as I have been calling it, Keats's conception of aestheticism. It is not exclusively an idea about the function of poetry, but about the function of all beauty in human life. That is why Keats does not equate the vast idea and "the end and aim of Poesy," but rather suggests that the latter is derived from the former: "*thence* too I've seen / The end and aim of Poesy" (emphasis mine). But the two are intimately related, and the suggestion that the vast idea is "manifest / As a large cross, some old cathedral's crest" leaves little doubt that Keats considered his vast idea a new alternative to traditional religion.

Accordingly, his dedication to the idea displays all the passionate intensity of a newly converted zealot:

> Therefore should I
> Be but the essence of deformity,
> A coward, did my very eye-lids wink
> At speaking out what I have dared to think.
> Ah! rather let me like a madman run
> Over some precipice; let the hot sun
> Melt my Dedalian wings, and drive me down
> Convuls'd and headlong!   (lines 297–304)

There is even the implication in Keats's address to poesy that this vast idea, like the poetry in which it will issue, has been mysteriously vouchsafed to him as a kind of revelation:

> And many a verse from so strange influence
> That we must ever wonder how, and whence
> It came.   (lines 69–71)

The saints of this new religion are the poets and artists. "So now," Keats concludes a letter to Haydon six months later, "in the Name of Shakespeare Raphael and all our Saints I commend you to the care of heaven!" And he signs the letter to this devout Christian friend with a final religious pun: "Your everlasting friend John Keats" (*Letters,* 1:145). Although he was painfully aware of his limitations and inexperience, the twenty-one-year-old poet desperately wanted to be among the sainthood, and all the more so since he now conceived a function for poetry that was even more urgent in a godless world:

> And they shall be accounted poet kings
> Who simply tell the most heart-easing things.
> O may these joys be ripe before I die.
> (lines 267–69)

Keats vowed that he would "strive / Against all doubtings" (lines 159–60), but he knew that fulfilling his own poetic program would require time. Consequently, there is a great emphasis on potential in "Sleep and Poetry," on the extraordinary possibilities of life and poetry. "Life is the rose's hope while yet unblown" (line 90), and poetry is "might half slumb'ring on its own right arm" (line 237). Keats realizes "how much toil" and "what desperate turmoil" (lines 307–8) will be required to explore the "widenesses" (line 309) stretching before him, but he retains the same religious sense of awe at the worlds he sees that "Cortez"'s men displayed when they "looked at each other with a wild surmise— / Silent, upon a peak in Darien."[5]

Despite his confidence, however, the highest kind of poetry must remain only a distant possibility for Keats at this stage in his career. Before he could move on to "the agonies, the strife / Of human hearts" (lines 124–25), he must pass ten years in the realm of "Flora, and old Pan" (line 102). Later I want to demonstrate how this distinction between what I have called "romance" or "pastoral" on the one hand and "tragedy" on the other—plainly a substantive rather than a formal distinction—becomes blurred in Keats's poetry almost from the beginning. Nonetheless, it remains a distinction which must be taken very seriously.

In the first place, this distinction is closely related to both the metaphor of the "Mansion of Many Apartments" and the argument in the "vale of Soul-making" letter that suffering is absolutely necessary to that full realization of human identity which Keats so cherished. Obviously Keats is being disingenuous when he implies in the epigraph to "Sleep and Poetry" that he has led an exceptionally carefree life, with neither "sicknesse nor disese." But the epigraph is not wholly ironic, since it underlines the relative innocence which Keats regarded as the central justification for his lengthy sojourn in the pretragic world of Flora and Pan. If he is to write poetry about the agonies of the human heart, he first must learn more about life, since "nothing," as he tells George and Georgiana, "ever becomes real till it is experienced" (*Letters*, 2:81).

This concern explains Keats's repeated determination to pursue knowledge, by which he mainly meant not abstract or philosophical knowledge but human knowledge, the kind of understanding of human life for which he lavishly praised and carefully reread Shakespeare.[6] "I am three and twenty with little knowledge and middling intellect," he tells Haydon in 1819. "It is true that in the height of enthusiasm I have been cheated into some fine passages, but that is nothing" (*Letters*, 2:43). In view of the fact that he had already written some of the greatest poetry in English, our tendency is to pass off this remark (together with similar ones expressing extreme skepticism about the value of all poetry) as either false modesty, frustration over the unenthusiastic reception of his poetry, or simply bad critical judgment. But in fact such statements reveal how zealously Keats regarded his task of acquiring knowledge as a necessary part of his poetic program. "I know nothing," he tells John Taylor, "and I mean to follow Solomon's directions of 'get Wisdom—get understanding'" (*Letters*, 1:271). For Keats the highest beauty requires both intensity of perception and assimilation of knowledge. Consequently, the "continual drinking of Knowledge" becomes analogous to a religious duty for Keats: "there is no worthy pursuit but the idea of doing some good for the world," he says; and then, after listing a number of possible ways of doing good, he concludes that "there is but one way for me—the road lies th[r]ough application study and thought" (*Letters*, 1:271).

But Keats's intense awareness of the limitations of his knowledge and experience could not extinguish his burning sense of poetic purpose. Whatever doubts he expresses relate not to the validity or propriety of "the end and aim of Poesy" but only to his ability properly and adequately to serve that end. He is, he says in "Sleep and Poetry," like those "who athirst to gain / A noble end, are thirsty every hour" (lines 282–83). Having seen with utter clarity the vast idea, the shining end and guiding principle of his life's work, Keats says: "I glean / Therefrom my liberty" (lines 291–92). By "liberty," I take it, he means freedom to go his own way, to pursue this new vast idea. "Will not some say that I presumptuously / Have spoken?" he asks (lines 270–71). Keats recognizes the immensity of his claim for a new religious function for poetry, and he underlines his confidence in what he has "dared to think" (line 300) by identifying with the most famous mythical figure of artistic pride. Should he fail to proclaim boldly what he believes, Keats says:

> let the hot sun
> Melt my Dedalian wings, and drive me down
> Convuls'd and headlong!   (lines 302–4)

Earlier in the poem Keats attacks the neoclassical poets and the other romantics for

> forgetting the great end
> Of poesy, that it should be a friend
> To sooth the cares, and lift the thoughts of man.
>   (lines 245–47)

77

The sin of the neoclassicists was didacticism, a poetry of

> musty laws lined out with wretched rule
> And compass vile: so that ye taught a school
> Of dolts to smooth, inlay, and clip, and fit.
> (lines 195–97)

By thus pretending to such a systematic understanding of life, these poets demonstrated that "irritable reaching after fact & reason" which is at odds with the ideal of Negative Capability, by virtue of which "with a great poet the sense of Beauty overcomes every other consideration, or rather obliterates all consideration" (*Letters*, 1:193–94). Thus it was only "the mask / Of Poesy" (lines 200–201) that these poets wore, and it blinded them to the poet's most important concern:

> The blue
> Bared its eternal bosom, and the dew
> Of summer nights collected still to make
> The morning precious: beauty was awake!
> Why were ye not awake? But ye were dead
> To things ye knew not of. (lines 189–94)

The romantic poetry of his own day comes under less fire. "Now 'tis a fairer season," Keats says, "for sweet music has been heard / In many places" (lines 221, 223–24). In the lake poets and in Hunt, Keats hears "fine sounds . . . floating wild / About the earth" (lines 228–29). Nonetheless, though "these things are doubtless" (line 230), romantic poetry has been a mixed blessing. "Mingled indeed with what is sweet and strong" (line 232) has been another variety of didacticism, a poetry in which

> the themes
> Are ugly clubs, the Poets Polyphemes
> Disturbing the grand sea. (lines 233–35)

What Keats is attacking here and in the following lines is "the wordsworthian or egotistical sublime" (*Letters*, 1:387).[7]

78

"It may be said that we ought to read our Contemporaries," Keats wrote to Reynolds in 1818:

> that Wordsworth &c should have their due from us. but for the sake of a few fine imaginative or domestic passages, are we to be bullied into a certain Philosophy engendered in the whims of an Egotist—Every man has his speculations, but every man does not brood and peacock over them till he makes a false coinage and deceives himself—Many a man can travel to the very bourne of Heaven, and yet want confidence to put down his halfseeing. Sancho will invent a Journey heavenward as well as any body. We hate poetry that has a palpable design upon us—and if we do not agree, seems to put its hand in its breeches pocket. Poetry should be great & unobtrusive, a thing which enters into one's soul, and does not startle it or amaze it with itself but with its subject.—How beautiful are the retired flowers! how would they lose their beauty were they to throng into the highway crying out, "admire me I am a violet! dote upon me I am a primrose!   (*Letters*, 1:223–24)

I quote this letter at length because it perfectly illustrates Keats's passionate opposition to the attempt of any poetry, not just Wordsworth's, to impose a particular philosophy on its readers. Everyone has his speculations, but (and here the hiatus in Keats's argument must be filled by his assumption of radical skepticism) since "nothing in this world is proveable" (*Letters*, 1:242), poetry should not occupy itself with these speculations. If no one can have certain knowledge of metaphysical matters, it must be a deception to elevate our private speculations to general truths. Instead, poetry should focus on the beauty of its subject, for if beauty is the only truth man can and needs to know, it must always be the first consideration of a great poet.

Byron too has forgotten this, and therefore he too comes under attack:

> But strength alone though of the Muses born
> Is like a fallen angel: trees uptorn,

79

Darkness, and worms, and shrouds, and sepulchres
Delight it; for it feeds upon the burrs,
And thorns of life.   (lines 241–45)

The first three cantos of *Childe Harold* had already appeared, and in these lines Keats seems to be objecting not only to the Gothic delight in darkness but also to the gloomy introspection and Titanic defiance of that poem, seeing them as still another form of poetic self-absorption, just one more "Philosophy engendered in the whims of an Egotist." Consequently, in that same letter, Keats says that he expects very little pleasure from the forthcoming "4th Book of Childe Harold & the whole of any body's life & opinions" (*Letters*, 1:225).

Underlying both this statement and the objection to Wordsworth's egotism is Keats's belief that the poet should aim not at self-expression but at selflessness. Against the notion of "the wordsworthian or egotistical sublime" Keats opposes the ideal of the "poetical Character," which "has no self," which "has no Identity" (*Letters*, 1:386–87). Hazlitt's critique of Wordsworth and Hazlitt's ideas about the objective poet and the related concept of sympathetic imagination exercised a powerful influence on Keats, which we see not only in Keats's idea of the poetical character but also in his conceptions of "disinterestedness" and Negative Capability. But for our purposes, the influence of Hazlitt, which has been long acknowledged, is less important than the skeptical assumptions that apparently led Keats to assimilate Hazlitt's ideas and to adapt them to his own developing conception of the function of poetry.[8] Keats expresses little interest in *Childe Harold* or "the whole of any body's life & opinions" because he regards self-expression as a mistaken ideal for poetry.

Although for Keats the necessity to remain in "uncertainties, Mysteries, doubts" about metaphysical questions is inevitable, his willingness to do so stems from this larger and more important certainty about the nature of the human situation and the great power of beauty and poetry. He rejects didactic and dogmatically philosophical poetry because in their reliance on metaphysics they are necessarily arbitrary, probably false, and most important of all, not truly consoling. The real poet recognizes human limitations and thus writes, as Keats says in "Sleep and Poetry," only about what "was for our human senses fitted" (line 80). I will, he says, "write on my tablets all that was permitted" (line 79), which, as the word *tablets* suggests, is material enough for a new kind of religious calling.

Keats describes the new poetry that he envisages in terms of a flower imagery that is remarkably reminiscent of "Written in Disgust of Vulgar Superstition," with its prediction that "fresh flowers will grow" on the ashes of Christianity, "and many glories of immortal stamp" (lines 13–14). After criticizing the poetry of his older contemporaries, he declares that there is still hope:

> Yet I rejoice: a myrtle fairer than
> E'er grew in Paphos, from the bitter weeds
> Lifts its sweet head into the air, and feeds
> A silent space with ever sprouting green.
> All tenderest birds there find a pleasant screen,
> Creep through the shade with jaunty fluttering,
> Nibble the little cupped flowers and sing.
> Then let us clear away the choking thorns
> From round its gentle stem; let the young fawns,
> Yeaned in after times, when we are flown,
> Find a fresh sward beneath it, overgrown
> With simple flowers.   (lines 248–59)

The "choking thorns" of poetic egotism must be cleared away from the "gentle stem" of Poesy, so that the newly emerging "simple flowers" may blossom and flourish and perform with their beauty the life-giving function of consolation.

By suggesting that the poetry of the agony and strife of

human hearts is "nobler" (line 123) than that of Flora and old Pan, Keats implies that it is also more consoling, since later in the poem he uses another hierarchical image to describe poetry: "And they shall be accounted poet *kings* / Who simply tell the most heart-easing things" (lines 267–68; emphasis mine). To contend that tragedy is nobler than romance and then to identify the highest poetry as that which is most consoling is to suggest that tragedy is more consoling as well. The paradox of this position is closely related to the "Melancholy" ode's conception of sorrow as prerequisite to the most consoling beauty; to the vale of soul-making's argument that suffering is necessary to the development of the soul; and to Keats's reference in "Hyperion" to "sorrow more beautiful than Beauty's self" (1. 36). Tragedy is more profoundly consoling than romance because it is based on a more inclusive view of life than the partial and sometimes evasive vision of romance.

But in "Sleep and Poetry," as elsewhere, Keats never suggests that the poetry of romance does not also console. To suggest that tragedy is more beautiful than romance is not to imply a condemnation of the latter. While Keats believed romance could not offer the more effective kind of consolation that tragedy could, he was never so gravely unrealistic as to deny the need for, and comforting effect of, occasional escapist release. For Keats, the problem with escapism is not that it is somehow wrong or deplorable in itself, but that it is ultimately less effective than other means of dealing with a painful world. But that is not to deny either the natural human need for occasional escape or its consolatory possibilities, however limited these may be. The only kind of escape that Keats condemns, in life as in literature, is that which continuously holds out as truth an idealized and false vision of the world, which can only lead to disillusionment and unhappiness. But the occasional retreat into romance which is undertaken with full knowledge of its limitations is harmless. Its immediate end may be escape from suffering, but to the extent that it consoles without deceiving, it serves a reconciling function which Keats would never condemn.

It is this last kind of romance that Keats has in mind when he speaks of the realm of Flora and old Pan in "Sleep and Poetry." It is the kind of poetry that is undertaken with full recognition of its limitations and its inferiority to the tragic poetry of the human heart. He knows that life is tragic:

> Stop and consider! life is but a day;
> A fragile dew-drop on its perilous way
> From a tree's summit; a poor Indian's sleep
> While his boat hastens to the monstrous steep
> Of Montmorenci.   (lines 85–89)

But he makes a conscious and undeceived decision to think of the beautiful aspects of life and deal with those in poetry:

>   Why so sad a moan?
> Life is the rose's hope while yet unblown;
> The reading of an ever-changing tale;
> The light uplifting of a maiden's veil;
> A pigeon tumbling in clear summer air;
> A laughing school-boy, without grief or care,
> Riding the springy branches of an elm.
>   (lines 89–95)

The decision is similar, in its undeceived hopefulness, to that of Milton in "Lycidas," when he invites the flowers to "strew the Laureate Hearse where Lycid lies" (line 151). Milton knows full well the ultimate inadequacy of this pagan ritual, but he temporarily indulges it for a bit of comfort: "For so to interpose a little ease, / Let our frail thoughts dally with false surmise" (lines 152–53).[9] Keats makes a similar decision in the sonnet "Oh! how I love," in which the retreat into an idealized nature and romance is not genuinely escapist, since it is undertaken with complete awareness of its limitations:

> Oh! how I love, on a fair summer's eve,
>   When streams of light pour down the golden west,

And on the balmy zephyrs tranquil rest
The silver clouds, far—far away to leave
All meaner thoughts, and take a sweet reprieve
 From little cares; to find, with easy quest,
 A fragrant wild, with Nature's beauty drest,
And there into delight my soul deceive.
There warm my breast with patriotic lore,
 Musing on Milton's fate—on Sydney's bier—
 Till their stern forms before my mind arise:
Perhaps on wing of Poesy upsoar,
 Full often dropping a delicious tear,
  When some melodious sorrow spells mine eyes.

Romance, or a certain kind of romance, performs the same function as sleep does. It refreshes and soothes us; it provides a temporary respite from the cares of life, a kind of "bower," to use one of Keats's favorite images, where we may pass a moment and come back with renewed spirits. Sleep, bowers, and poetry are all closely connected in Keats's mind and imagery. When a poet writes a poem, he is making permanent a fleeting beauty of life, so that we can return to it, as to a bower, for consolation. That, I think, is what Keats means when he says in the famous opening line of *Endymion*, "A thing of beauty is a joy forever," or when he tells Rice that Milton was "an active friend to Man all his Life and has been since his death" (*Letters*, 1:255). Keats's notion of the immortality of art has nothing mystical or arcane or otherworldly about it; he means by it simply that a work of art can continue to give pleasure and consolation even after its creator has died. This is, in fact, one of poetry or art's special advantages over many other forms of beauty: it is permanently available. I think Keats has exactly this sense in mind in both "Ode on a Grecian Urn" and "Sleep and Poetry," where he hopes that he can "find out an immortality" (line 84). Nor is it merely poetry that has the capacity to function as a bower. "You will preserve all my Letters," Keats tells his sister, "and I will secure yours

—and thus in the course of time we shall each of us have a good Bundle—which, hereafter, when things may have strangely altered and god knows what happened, we may read over together and look with pleasure on times past— that now are to come" (*Letters,* 1:156).[10]

iii

I think it is no exaggeration to say that Keats never did write poetry of a purely escapist sort. He did, of course, write many romances, but all of them, even the earliest ones, demonstrate an awareness of tragic reality. The most brilliant example, "The Eve of St. Agnes," celebrates a moment of intensity by framing romance in tragedy. The problem of escape itself becomes the subject of a number of Keats's poems—notably "La Belle Dame," "Ode to a Nightingale," "Lamia," and *The Fall of Hyperion.* Despite Keats's distinction, then, between what I have called romance or pastoral on the one hand and tragedy on the other, his poetry showed healthy signs of tragedy's intrusion almost from the beginning. Even in early poems, like *Endymion* or "Imitation of Spenser" (which is probably his first poem), there is a quite unsentimental undersense of transience and pain.[11] In the "Imitation of Spenser" Keats argues what was to become his familiar conception of poetry as consolation:

> Ah! could I tell the wonders of an isle
> That in that fairest lake had placed been,
> I could e'en Dido of her grief beguile;
> Or rob from aged Lear his bitter teen.
> (lines 19–22)

And at the beginning of *Endymion* Keats tells us that beauty works to alleviate suffering and thus reconcile us to life:

> on every morrow, are we wreathing
> A flowery band to bind us to the earth,
> Spite of despondence, of the inhuman dearth

85

> Of noble natures, of the gloomy days,
> Of all the unhealthy and o'er-darkened ways
> Made for our searching: yes, in spite of all,
> Some shape of beauty moves away the pall
> From our dark spirits.   (1. 6–13)

Although he never did write purely escapist romance, Keats still felt, in "Sleep and Poetry," that he was not yet ready to move out of his own version of the realm of Flora and old Pan to the "nobler life" (line 123) of tragic poetry. While he has an expansive and liberating sense of the paradoxically consolatory possibilities of tragic poetry, he sees that enterprise only "in long perspective" (line 100), for he believes he does not yet have the necessary knowledge and experience to undertake such a crucially important task. It is not that he has had insufficient contact with the agony and strife of human hearts; he clearly has, and its impact has already been felt in his poetry. "But vain is now the burning and the strife," as he says a year later in "On Seeing a Lock of Milton's Hair": "Pangs are in vain, until I grow high-rife / With old Philosophy" (lines 29–31). Again, "Philosophy" here has its most common Keatsian meaning of wisdom, or knowledge of human life, and it is this that, in "Sleep and Poetry," Keats feels he lacks:

> What though I am not wealthy in the dower
> Of spanning wisdom; though I do not know
> The shiftings of the mighty winds that blow
> Hither and thither all the changing thoughts
> Of man: though no great minist'ring reason sorts
> Out the dark mysteries of human souls
> To clear conceiving.   (lines 284–90)

Still, he says, though all this may be true—though his experience and abilities may still be limited—he knows exactly what poetry must do. There is a remarkable similarity between this sentiment and that which Keats expresses in the preface to *Endymion*:

Knowing within myself the manner in which this Poem has been produced, it is not without a feeling of regret that I make it public.

What manner I mean, will be quite clear to the reader, who must soon perceive great inexperience, immaturity, and every error denoting a feverish attempt, rather than a deed accomplished. . . . the foundations are too sandy. It is just that this youngster should die away: a sad thought for me, if I had not some hope that while it is dwindling I may be plotting, and fitting myself for verses fit to live.

This may be speaking too presumptuously . . . but . . . there is not a fiercer hell than the failure in a great object. This is not written with the least atom of purpose to forestall criticisms . . . but from the desire I have to conciliate men who are competent to look, and who do look with a zealous eye, to the honour of English literature.

We find in this preface that same revealing combination of self-criticism and self-confidence that characterizes "Sleep and Poetry." Keats is fully cognizant of the great gap in *Endymion* between his intention and his accomplishment, and it is, he tells us, a result of "inexperience, immaturity." But although the foundations in his own life and experience are as yet "too sandy," he knows that he has had "a great object" in mind. If his inexperience in life and in the writing of poetry has made the present work a failure, he at least can be confident that his poetic program is the right one and that eventually he might make "verses fit to live."

Despite his deep sense of his own limitations, Keats knew he must throw himself totally into poetry and not sit around waiting for maturity. "If I do hide myself," he writes in "Sleep and Poetry,"

> it sure shall be
> In the very fane, the light of Poesy:
> If I do fall, at least I will be laid
> Beneath the silence of a poplar shade.
> (lines 275–78)

Although he ultimately realized how flawed *Endymion* was, he took the poem extremely seriously, recognizing all the time that he was working within the limits of his experience:

> J. S. is perfectly right in regard to the slipshod Endym-
> ion. That it is so is no fault of mine.—No!—though it
> may sound a little paradoxical. It is as good as I had
> power to make it—by myself. . . . The Genius of
> Poetry . . . cannot be matured by law & precept, but by
> sensation & watchfulness in itself. . . . In Endymion, I
> leaped headlong into the Sea, and thereby have become
> better acquainted with the Soundings, the quicksands,
> & the rocks, than if I had stayed upon the green shore,
> and piped a silly pipe, and took tea and comfortable
> advice.—I was never afraid of failure; for I would
> sooner fail than not be among the greatest.
>
> *(Letters,* 1:374)

Always for Keats, even in his own self-analysis, ideals are firmly rooted in realities, and magnificently ambitious possibilities are squarely grounded in a clearheaded sense of the limitations that bound them.

Endymion was Keats's first major attempt to realize his vast idea—"a test," as he wrote to Bailey, "a trial of my Powers of Imagination" (*Letters,* 1:169). As such, we must take the poem as seriously as Keats did, recognizing with him its flaws but, more important, trying to determine why it was that he devoted such immense energy to this strangely enigmatic and extremely ambitious poem. *Endymion* is in fact an excellent test case for the new view of Keats's work which I have been proposing. Any inclusive interpretation of Keats which cannot accommodate a poem which he took so seriously is probably itself inadequate.

———

"Wherein lies happiness?" When Keats sent his publisher

the famous revised lines that begin with this question, he told him that having written this passage "will perhaps be of the greatest Service to me of any thing I ever did" (*Letters*, 1:218). Whether or not Keats was right, the question itself suggests the fundamental problem with which all of his poetry is concerned: Given the inevitability of suffering and uncertainty about higher reality, how can men be happy? *Endymion* addresses this question in a diffuse and often perplexing way, but its essential answer is consistent with that which Keats provides throughout the rest of his work: Happiness is limited, but it can be achieved by avoiding false ideals and embracing those that bind one to earthly reality without enslaving one in a merely sensual existence.

Endymion eventually learns through experience what he knows only abstractly in the "fellowship with essence" passage (1. 777ff.), and thus proves the Keatsian observation that "Nothing ever becomes real till it is experienced" (*Letters*, 2:81). In this sense, *Endymion* is a kind of *Bildungsroman,* but it is also an allegory, as numerous commentators have pointed out, about the development of a poet and the function of poetry. Many critics who have read the poem allegorically have done so along Neoplatonic lines, and have thus seen the plot as expressing the poet's desire for and eventual merging with some kind of higher reality or ideal beauty. The assumption that Keats believed in any such reality, let alone made it the subject of his allegory, seems to me as mistaken as the view that the poem is not an allegory at all—a position that a number of critics have taken up largely in reaction to the Neoplatonic reading.[12] It is rather from the broad perspective of the question, "Wherein lies happiness?" that *Endymion* concerns itself with the function of poetry. Since poetry must be based on and affirm the same values that promote happiness in life, Endymion's allegorical journey through deception to discovery of those values represents the poet's quest for the foundations of a poetry that can itself truly serve human happiness.

—————

The epigraph to *Endymion,* which is a line from Shakespeare's seventeenth sonnet, raises many of the crucial issues with which the poem will concern itself. Here is the Shakespearean sonnet from which the line comes:

> Who will believe my verse in time to come
> If it were filled with your most high deserts?
> Though yet, Heaven knows, it is but as a tomb
> Which hides your life and shows not half your parts.
> If I could write the beauty of your eyes
> And in fresh numbers number all your graces,
> The age to come would say, "This poet lies;
> Such heavenly touches ne'er touched earthly faces."
> So should my papers, yellowed with their age,
> Be scorned, like old men of less truth than tongue,
> And your true rights be termed a poet's rage
> And stretched meter of an antique song.
>> But were some child of yours alive that time,
>> You should live twice, in it and in my rhyme.

Keats, like Shakespeare in this sonnet, is extremely concerned about the credibility of his poem: "Who will believe my verse in time to come?" The question is an especially gnawing one for the writer of romance, for he faces the same charge of excessive idealization that Shakespeare anticipates as a result of praising his beloved: "This poet lies; / Such heavenly touches ne'er touched earthly faces." Keats too will be concerned in *Endymion* with this contrast between heavenly and earthly, particularly in terms of human limitations and possibilities. Like Shakespeare, he will investigate the relationship between beauty and truth, fully aware that the problem of romance is to avoid a complete disjunction between the two, lest the poem "be scorned, like old men of less truth than tongue," i.e., of less truth than

eloquence. And finally, like Shakespeare, Keats's concern
with telling the truth of the human condition has a decidedly historical dimension. "In time to come," after the poet has
died and future generations have come and gone, will his
poem be regarded merely as the "stretched meter of an antique song," an irrelevant remnant of an archaically idealis-
tic view of humanity? But like Shakespeare in the final
couplet, Keats hopes his poem will achieve an immortality,
so that its vision can in fact live on "in my rhyme."

The opening lines of book 1 implicitly confirm this hope:

> A thing of beauty is a joy for ever:
> Its loveliness increases; it will never
> Pass into nothingness; but still will keep
> A bower quiet for us, and a sleep
> Full of sweet dreams, and health, and quiet breathing.
>
> (1. 1–5)

Beautiful things can avoid oblivion by living on in the
memory as a quiet bower to which one can return. The special claim of poetry, like all art, is that by isolating moments
of beauty from the flux of time, it too can serve as a bower,
an immortalized place to which one can retire for periodic
renewal. One is immediately reminded of "Sleep and Poetry" in these lines, and the suggestion that like sleep, poetry
can refresh us. Here Keats extends the comparison to all
things of beauty and introduces his favorite image of the
bower.

Keats uses this image in several of his poems, but never
so extensively or effectively as in *Endymion*. Just after Endymion is introduced, staring woefully in a trance of grief,
his sister Peone takes him off "towards a bowery island" to
comfort him:

> she steered light
> Into a shady, fresh, and ripply cove,
> Where nested was an arbour, overwove
> By many a summer's silent fingering;

> To whose cool bosom she was used to bring
> Her playmates, with their needle broidery,
> And minstrel memories of times gone by.
>
> (1. 428–35)

The bower is thus associated both with consolation and with poetry, the "minstrel memories of times gone by." As Endymion rests, Peone speaks an apostrophe to sleep:

> O magic sleep! O comfortable bird
> That broodest o'er the troubled sea of the mind
> Till it is hush'd and smooth! O unconfin'd
> Restraint! imprisoned liberty! great key
> To golden palaces, strange minstrelsy,
> . . . .
>   aye, to all the mazy world
> Of silvery enchantment!—who, upfurl'd
> Beneath thy drowsy wing a triple hour,
> But renovates and lives?—Thus, in the bower,
> Endymion was calm'd to life again.
>
> (1. 453–57, 461–64)

Magically, like poetry and all other forms of beauty, sleep heals and refreshes. As a result of his short sleep "in the bower, / Endymion was calm'd to life again."

Later, in book 2, the young prince fears the return of the melancholy loneliness which had earlier stung him so severely. Alone in "a jasmine bower" (2. 670), he therefore implores the aid of sleep:

> hither, Sleep, awhile!
> Hither, most gentle Sleep! and soothing foil
> For some few hours the coming solitude.
>
> (2. 704–6)

Here again, sleep is regarded as a temporary bower that can nerve one up for coming sorrow. For Glaucus, whose situation parallels Endymion's in many ways, it was the bowers themselves, rather than sleep, that provided a refuge against his suffering, but the association with sleep is present there too:

Rough billows were my home by night and day,—
The sea-gulls not more constant; for I had
No housing from the storm and tempests mad,
But hollow rocks,—and they were palaces
Of silent happiness, of slumberous ease.

(3. 320–24)

The discovery of some "housing from the storm," some
place of refuge where he could temporarily rest in "silent
happiness," was for Glaucus literally a matter of life and
death. For Keats, as I have already pointed out, it was
spiritually nothing less. Things of beauty "alway must be
with us, or we die" (1. 33). That is why it is only the intervention of Diana, as the spirit of beauty, that can save Endymion from death as the result of the despair he feels after
seeing the morbid and decaying relics at the bottom of the
sea:

and unless
Dian had chaced away that heaviness,
He might have died: but now, with cheered feel,
He onward kept.   (3. 137–40)

The dialectic of earthly/transcendent, real/ideal, and mor-
tal/immortal serves exactly the same purpose in *Endymion*
that the religious context serves in "Sleep and Poetry," or
the use of the term *soul* serves in the "vale of Soul-making"
letter. The list of parallel examples is long and is worth
pausing over a moment and noticing how many of Keats's
most famous poems and letters it includes. In addition to
"Sleep and Poetry" and *Endymion,* there is the "finer tone"
letter, with its use of *heaven* and *here after,* and the "Mansion of Many Apartments" letter, with (as we shall soon see)
its adaptation of a biblical simile and its use of the word
providence and the imagery of wine and bread. In "The Eve
of St. Agnes," "Ode on Melancholy," "Ode to Psyche," and
the two "Hyperion" poems the principle of contrast that
underlies all these other instances (including "Lamia," "La

93

Belle Dame," and "Ode to a Nightingale") moves into the foreground, since Keats is concerned in these later poems with directly contrasting his new religion with earlier, more illusory ones. At a structural level, we see the same technique operating in the letter on "real, semireal, and no things," and in the famous claim of the Grecian urn that "Beauty is truth, truth beauty." For in both of those cases Keats purposely employs a metaphysical vocabulary in order to express a decidedly antimetaphysical view. In *Endymion*, then, the spiritual significance that has traditionally been associated with the transcendent, ideal, and immortal is transferred to the earthly, real, and mortal.

Keats uses this technique in order to accommodate his humanized religion to the historical realities of his age and to redefine the spiritual. But that is only one reason why Keats uses the dialectic of earthly/transcendent, real/ideal, and mortal/immortal in *Endymion*. The other reason is timeless rather than historical, for he sees the religious impulse as permanently characteristic of the human heart, an *"a-priori* category," as the modern German religious historian Rudolf Otto has called it, a *"predisposition"* or *"religious impulsion"* which originates in "the obscure *a-priori* foundation of thought itself." The "religious root," says Paul Tillich, is in some cases "carefully covered, in others . . . passionately denied; in some it is deeply hidden and in others superficially. But it is never completely absent."[13] Keats thought that this universal religious impulse usually took the form of believing or yearning to believe in some extra-human reality—transcendent truth, ideal beauty, or immortality. Tillich, like most Christian theologians, believed that the impulse could only be satisfied by belief in such a reality. But according to Keats, as *Endymion* demonstrates, the proper fulfillment of the religious impulse in an enlightened age lies not in the transcendent but in the human realm.

Thus one side of Keats's view that the story of *Endymion* illustrates is the natural human desire for transcendent reality, the disillusioning and destructive effects of belief in such a reality, the discovery of its falsehood, and the eventual recognition that human happiness can result only from the full acceptance, indeed embracing, of the earthly, mortal condition. For when properly viewed, this condition is seen to possess the spiritual possibilities that had formerly been connected with its opposite: the transcendent and ideal. The significance of Cynthia turning out to be identical with the Indian Maiden is not that transcendent reality can only be apprehended through earthly reality, or that physical, sensual reality is all that exists; it is, rather, that earthly, human reality itself comes to be spiritualized. The source of spirituality has been transferred or displaced from heaven to earth, because human reality is seen to have within it the "principle of beauty" and thus the possibility of a new kind of spirituality—the holiness of the human heart.

Dramatically, however, the choice presents itself as a duality. Endymion must choose between the earthly and the transcendent, between the Indian Maiden and Dian. At the beginning of the poem, he has renounced his active life in the world of men (emphasized by the fact that he is a prince) in order to pursue, as Peona puts it, "things mysterious, / Immortal, starry" (1. 506–7). He has had a vision, a magnificent dream of ideal beauty in which "the doors / Of heaven appear'd to open for my flight" (1. 581–82):

> Whence that completed form of all completeness?
> Whence came that high perfection of all sweetness?
> Speak, stubborn earth, and tell me where, O where
> Hast thou a symbol of her golden hair?   (1. 606–9)

There are no answers to these questions, for the vision of ideal beauty and perfection was too beautiful, too perfect to have either a source or an analogue in earthly experience. Endymion, although he still has a "dazzled soul" (1. 594),

first realizes the dangers of falling in love with an ideal un-
realizable on earth when he awakens from his dream and
discovers, like the knight in "La Belle Dame," that everything on earth that had been beautiful before is no longer so:

> all the pleasant hues
> Of heaven and earth had faded: deepest shades
> Were deepest dungeons; heaths and sunny glades
> Were full of pestilent light; our taintless rills
> Seem'd sooty, and o'er-spread with upturn'd gills
> Of dying fish; the vermeil rose had blown
> In frightful scarlet, and its thorns out-grown
> Like spiked aloe.   (1. 691–98)

Keats has chosen these images carefully: these shades and
rills and roses are meant to remind us of the earlier list of
beautiful things that he provided in the proem as examples
of what "bind[s] us to the earth" and consoles us. Endymion,
having renounced earthly for transcendent ideals, has thereby cut himself off from the true source of beauty and can
thus expect nothing but this endless cycle of bliss and despair.

Yet Endymion is never wholly oblivious to earthly joys or
to what he has lost. Twice when he describes his dream to
Peona he applies the word *mad* or *madly* to himself and his
actions (1. 613, 653), and after describing his rapacious attempts to preserve his bliss—so that it might be "plunder'd
of its load of blessedness" (1. 660)—he calls himself a "desperate mortal" (1. 661). He laments his inability to be consoled by earthly beauties, until finally, "Time, that aged
nurse, / Rock'd me to patience" (1. 705–6):

> Now, thank gentle heaven!
> These things, with all their comfortings, are given
> To my down-sunken hours, and with thee,
> Sweet sister, help to stem the ebbing sea
> Of weary life.   (1. 706–10)

It is this kind of essential understanding that allows Endymion to perceive the correct answer to his own question, "Wherein lies happiness?" (1. 777), despite the fact that he still suffers under the delusion of a belief in transcendent reality. In this way, Keats can demonstrate both the stubborn human desire for belief in a higher reality and the fact that understanding can never be complete until it has been borne out by experience. Nonetheless, Endymion's answer to "Wherein lies happiness?" clearly reflects Keats's own answer to the question that underlies all his work.

Happiness, Endymion tells us, is to be found

> In that which becks
> Our ready minds to fellowship divine,
> A fellowship with essence. (1. 777–79)

I take "fellowship with essence" to mean that condition in which we perceive "the principle of beauty in all things." Keats uses the word *essences* in the proem to *Endymion* (1. 25) to refer to things of beauty as they are perceived qua beauty. Essences are, as it were, what the imagination distills out of reality—from real things, semireal things, and no things alike—and presents to the experiencing consciousness as beauty.

As a result of such fellowship, "we shine, / Full alchemiz'd, and free of space" (1. 779–80). This kind of chemical vocabulary, which we find throughout Keats's poems and letters, has been elaborately analyzed by Stuart Sperry, who rightly denies that the word *essence* in *Endymion* indicates, as the Neoplatonic critics would have it, "an affimation of belief in a Platonic or transcendental reality." "What has gone unnoticed," Sperry contends, "is the fact that it is the creative process the passage describes, and that the chief key to its significance . . . is its relation to chemical theory."[14] Sperry finds in the poems and letters a "consistent design to the metaphors [Keats] uses to describe the way the imagination operates upon its materials, the way it condenses and refines them into a higher state," which is what Keats means by "essences."[15] Sperry's explanation of Keats's imagery of consumption and digestion, spinning and weaving, fermentation, distillation, intensity, and various other such metaphors for the creative process, seems to me highly persuasive. But though he does not deny its broader significance, Sperry unduly emphasizes the purely poetic dimension of Keats's conception of the creative process. By thus slighting its more fundamental application to the nature of human perception, he obscures the more significant point that the creative process, like Keats's principle of aestheticism, is important to poetry in precisely the same way, and only to the extent, that it is important to life. The poet transforms his materials into beauty just as the man, through a creative act of perception, transforms the materials of reality into beauty.

What the chemical analogies provided Keats was not merely a way of "explaining the origin and operation of *poetry* as an immaterial or 'spiritual' power active throughout the universe," as Sperry contends, but a way of explaining the operation of *beauty*. It is not simply poetry, but the perception of beauty that "can be said to operate through the laws by which the mind, and more especially the imagination, assimilates and transmutes the impressions it derives from nature."[16] These distillations are what Keats means by "essences."

But there is a pregnant paradox here, and it is thrown into greater relief by a statement Keats makes in a letter to Bailey: "I have the same Idea of all our Passions as of love they are all in their sublime, creative of essential Beauty" (*Letters*, 1:184). But how can what is essential be created? The answer is that it is the special power of the imagination to make real for human consciousness that principle or potential for beauty which exists in all things. Keats does not base this idea on any kind of subtle or rarefied metaphysics, but rather on what he takes to be an empirical fact of human experience: that all things can be made beautiful to human consciousness if only they are properly perceived.

Happiness, then, lies in making contact with the essence of beauty; or, to state the matter in different terms, happiness is that condition which occurs when one imaginatively perceives beauty. There is nothing otherworldly about this notion; the essence of beauty is purely a matter of human perceptual intensity, and the imagination which enables us to perceive essential beauty does not thereby mediate some higher reality. Early in the poem, when Endymion calls the fellowship "divine," he probably means divine in a transcendent sense; but he learns in the course of the poem what Keats already knows when he writes these lines: fellowship "divine" refers not to a divinity beyond this world but to the way in which this purely human activity assumes the spiritual values of affirmation and consolation that had traditionally been thought available only by means of a relationship with the transcendent divine.

The "gradations of Happiness" which Keats then proceeds to outline turn out to be the familiar categories of beauty which we have already encountered in the proem and which recur again in another list of beauties in book 3: those of nature, of art, of mythology and religion, and of friendship and love. The "rose leaf" (1. 782) recalls the "fair musk-rose blooms" of 1. 19; the "old songs [which] waken from enclouded tombs" (1. 787) and the "Ghosts of melodious prophecyings" (1. 789) recall the religious myths of 1. 20–21, "the grandeur of the dooms / We have imagined for the mighty dead;" the "Bronze clarions" (1. 791) anticipate the "clarion's blast" of 3. 167; the lullabies associated with Orpheus (1. 793–94) look forward to the "poet's harp" of 3. 165; and the reference to friendship (1. 801ff.) anticipates "the voice of friends" of 3. 165. Unlike the letter on real, semireal, and no things, which sets out a gradation of beauty in terms of the degree of imagination necessary to perceive it, this is a gradation of "Happiness," "a kind of Pleasure Thermometer" (*Letters*, 1:218), in Keats's phrase, which describes a scale of the pleasure or happiness that results from beauty rather than the degree of imaginative intensity necessary to perceive or create that beauty in the first place.

At the top of this scale is love, the nature of which Endymion must and does discover in the course of his quest. Although he himself must face the issue as a choice between the heavenly and the earthly, he already realizes that the kind of love he has been describing here as "the tip-top" (1. 805) of happiness is earthly love (1. 843). But at this point he is still so soul-bedazzled that he deceives himself by reasoning that if mortal or earthly love can make men happy, how much happier must immortal or heavenly love make them:

> Now, if this earthly love has power to make
> Men's being mortal, immortal; to shake
> Ambition from their memories, and brim
> Their measure of content; what merest whim,
> Seems all this poor endeavor after fame,
> To one, who keeps within his steadfast aim
> A love immortal, an immortal too.
>
> (1. 843–49)

What Endymion will discover at the end of the poem is that this kind of reasoning is not only a deception but, more important, that it is also a cause of disillusionment and unhappiness. His journey will prove to him through experience what he already knows but cannot fully accept here: that the kind of love that leads to true happiness is human love, between two real, mortal people.

Friendship is one rung below love only because it lacks

the sexuality, and hence the intensified beauty and pleasure of human contact, that love involves. It hardly seems necessary to argue the crucial role of sexuality in this poem and its conception of love. Some critics, such as Ford and Pettet, have felt it necessary to stress the importance of sex in *Endymion* mainly to overturn the extravagantly Neoplatonic allegorical readings of other commentators, such as Finney or Thorpe. But these critics have often taken an equally exaggerated position, which, in its tendency to offer one extreme in place of another, recalls the polarization set up by Stillinger in reaction to Wasserman's reading of "The Eve of St. Agnes." "It would be wrong," as Sperry points out, "to imply that critics of [*Endymion*] have necessarily embraced one view or the other, the traditional [Neoplatonic] allegorical or the erotic. Nevertheless the two approaches have to date proved most influential and have polarized debate around certain questions of crucial importance."[17]

What both positions overlook is that Keats has appropriated the spiritual values normally associated with the Neoplatonic realm in order to spiritualize the purely human realm, for which sex serves at once as the most intense expression and the most appropriate metaphor. But unlike the mere sensuality of Circe, for example, it is a spiritualized sexuality which Keats celebrates here, as in "The Eve of St. Agnes." The influence of human love, Keats says, "genders a novel sense" (1. 808), and by "novel" Keats apparently means "of a new kind or nature." Love, that is to say, begets in one a sixth sense, a new kind of perception, which is the perception of beauty in all things. Love, we remember, is, like all the passions, paradoxically creative of essential beauty, and this paradox is again suggested in the lines that follow, which describe the process of "melting into" the "radiance" of love: "When we combine therewith / Life's self is nourish'd by its proper pith" (1. 810, 813–14). Human life, in other words, is spiritually nourished or developed by its "proper pith" or own stuff in the process of loving another human being.[18]

But Endymion must learn all this on his pulses. "Thou must wander far," the dream-goddess tells him:

> In other regions, past the scanty bar
> To mortal steps, before thou canst be ta'en
> From every wasting sigh, from every pain,
> Into the gentle bosom of thy love.
> Why it is thus, one knows in heaven above.
>
> (2. 123–28)

It is because life is so full of sighs and pains that human beings aspire to a higher condition where they hope to be free of miseries. But as Keats learns in "Ode to a Nightingale," the only reality from which human suffering is absent is death. Yet despite the impossibility of transcending the mortal condition, the urge to do so is deeply human. Although Keats comes out strongly, in *Endymion* as elsewhere, against submitting to the desire for transcendence, he recognizes its powerful attraction. Indeed, as Endymion's quest dramatizes, attempting to go beyond human limitations seems to be an extremely effective, if very painful, way of coming to realize the fiction of super-human reality and the need to embrace the human.

It seems to me only a half-truth (and a very misleading half-truth) to interpret the merging of Cynthia and the Indian Maiden as Keats's suggestion that ultimate, super-human reality cannot be known outside of human, earthly reality. This has been, with varying points of emphasis, the most common interpretation. According to C. L. Finney, for example, Keats is insisting that "the beauty of a particular woman is a manifestation of ideal or essential beauty." Douglas Bush, who finds the merging an unsatisfactory "equation in Platonic algebra, not an experience," argues that the fusion is meant to signify "the idea that the way to the One lies through loving apprehension of the Many." And Walter Evert thinks that the merging "confirms the whole point of Endymion's journeyings, the lesson that only by full sensitivity to and appreciation of the mundane can we come to apprehension of the divine, for they are inextricably mingled in human experience."[19]

All of these critics are right in emphasizing that transcendent reality cannot be known by itself. But they are wrong, I think, in assuming that Keats believes it can be known at all. The reason Keats sanctions "the beauty of a particular woman," or the "loving apprehension of the Many," or "full sensitivity to and appreciation of the mundane" is not to suggest that such human experience mediates "ideal . . . beauty," or "the One," or "the divine"; but rather to suggest that within itself it contains the life-giving spiritual values normally connected with ideal beauty, ultimate reality, and the divine. The difference is absolutely crucial, for Keats is not suggesting that the human mediates the divine but that it is itself divine.

What Endymion discovers is that the very urge for transcendence itself involves a dangerous illusion:

> There never liv'd a mortal man, who bent
> His appetite beyond his natural sphere,
> But starv'd and died. My sweetest Indian, here,
> Here will I kneel, for thou redeemed hast
> My life from too thin breathing: gone and past
> Are cloudy phantasms. Caverns lone, farewel!
> And air of visions, and the monstrous swell
> Of visionary seas! No, never more
> Shall airy voices cheat me to the shore
> Of tangled wonder, breathless and aghast.
>
> (4. 646–55)

I cannot agree with Evert's claim that "while these lines may constitute a first flash of insight into the attitude which became basic in Keats's later poetry, they are out of keeping with the aesthetic vision that *Endymion* exists to propagate."[20] The aesthetic vision of *Endymion* does not seem to me substantially different from the vision of Keats's later poetry. Far from violating the essential attitude of this poem, these words of Endymion represent the logical and dramatically appropriate conclusion of his quest. For he has been made to choose between earthly and heavenly love, and even before he is accorded the revelation of the identity of Cynthia with the Indian Maiden, he chooses the earthly and thus comes out on the same side of the question which he had earlier acknowledged in the "Wherein lies happiness" passage. The difference is that now he has shed his illusions about the possibilities of divine love and has learned on his pulses the truth of his earlier celebration of human love. The fact that Endymion wins Cynthia only after he has renounced her indicates not that the transcendent divine can be apprehended only by concentration on the human, but that only when one has given up the illusion of the transcendent and lovingly embraced the human can the latter disclose its rich potential for spirituality on its own terms rather than as a mediator of something beyond itself. Keats's conception of "happiness," then, is, as Abrams has suggested, the "secular version of the religious concept of 'felicity' which, in the orthodox view, is to be achieved by a surrender of oneself to God."[21]

Although it may seem odd, in a chapter mainly concerned with the function of poetry, to have dwelt so long on *Endymion*'s treatment of the values of life rather than art, I have done so intentionally in order to underscore, and I hope more clearly reveal, the crucial relationship between life and art which Keats wants to establish in *Endymion* as in so many of his other poems. It should by now be evident that Endymion's pursuit of Cynthia is, as Walter Evert has said, "the romance equivalent of the poet's pursuit of poetry. In this consists the whole basis of the poem's allegory."[22] Like Endymion, the poet must come to see that the true source of happiness lies in this and not some other world; that the only beauty humans can and need to know is human, not ideal, beauty; and that only when one recognizes the illusion of immortality and transcendent reality and embraces mortality will mortal experience disclose its spiritual fullness. The true poet will come to realize that his poetry must not only be based on this view of life, but that it must promote these human values and celebrate these intensities of mortal experience, of hope and desire and love, that will console man in a painful world. The poet must mediate an awareness of both the limits and the potentials of human knowledge and experience, and if he does that properly his poetry will reveal the same kind of truth that experience does: that beauty is the only truth we know and need to know.

That one may properly call such a view a religion of beauty seems to me supported by the fact that Keats again uses an abundance of religious language and imagery throughout the poem. Two examples should serve to illustrate its function. The first, Keats's description of Cynthia near the beginning of book 3, reminds us that Keats means to attach a religious significance to this mighty power of beauty:

> O moon! old boughs lisp forth a *holier* din
> The while they feel thine airy fellowship
> Thou dost *bless* every where, with silver lip
> Kissing dead things to life. The sleeping kine,
> Couched in thy brightness, dream of fields *divine*:
> Innumerable mountains rise, and rise,
> Ambitious for the *hallowing* of thine eyes;

And yet thy *benediction* passeth not
One obscure hiding-place, one little spot.
(3. 54–62; emphasis mine)

"The poetry of earth," we remember from "On the Grass-hopper and Cricket," "is never dead" (line 1). But it is the spirit of beauty which must kiss it into life and make it holy. This is why Keats tells Shelley to " 'load every rift' of your subject with ore" (*Letters*, 2:323). "*An artist*," he says, "must serve Mammon," by which he means "the Poetry, and dra-matic effect"—the poetic or local, textural beauty—rather than serve "God," by which he means some "purpose"—a philosophical system or didactic teaching (*Letters*, 2:322). Keats has again inverted the traditional religious scheme. His recommendation of Mammon instead of God is another way of transposing religious significance from heaven to earth, from divine to human.[23] This characteristic spirituali-zation of the secular has the effect of making the role of the poet and poetry religious: "My Imagination is a Monastry and I am its Monk—you must explain my metap^cs to your-self" (*Letters*, 2:323). The religious task of the poet is not to reveal anew the divine scheme of things but to create beauty from the materials of human experience. As Oceanus says in "Hyperion," "first in beauty should be first in might" (2. 229). The most powerful, the most effective poetry is simply that which is most beautiful, and the description of Cynthia in *Endymion* as "the gentlier-mightiest" (3. 43) reminds us that, as an allegorical figure, she too represents this same ideal.[24]

The second example of the association between Keats's religious imagery and his conception of beauty occurs in the Glaucus episode, which vividly dramatizes the poet's role as "physician to all men." By joining Glaucus as the necessary adjunct to that aged man's mysterious but sacred mission of resurrecting the lovers, Endymion renders a humane service which is all the more significant since such a high premium has been placed on love earlier in the poem. The numerous

parallels between Endymion and Glaucus scarcely need re-
hearsing. Together, these mutually reflective figures indicate
that the poet is an instrumental agent of human happiness,
and here again Keats uses religious language to emphasize
the nature of the enterprise. The lovers have been "enshrined
piously" (3. 721), and Endymion awakens them to the marvelous delights of divine-like harmony and luxury:

> Delicious symphonies, like airy flowers,
> Budded, and swell'd, and, full-blown, shed full showers
> Of light, soft, unseen leaves of sounds divine.
> The two deliverers tasted a pure wine
> Of happiness, from fairy-press ooz'd out.
> Speechless they eyed each other, and about
> The fair assembly wander'd to and fro,
> Distracted with the richest overflow
> Of joy that ever pour'd from heaven.
>
> (3. 798–806)

What happens to these lovers is what Endymion had earlier
wished for Alpheus and Arethusa:

> I urge
> Thee, gentle Goddess of my pilgrimage,
> By our eternal hopes, to soothe, to assuage,
> If thou art powerful, these lovers' pains;
> And make them happy in some happy plains.
>
> (2. 1013–17)

But the poet, for all his power to ease the burden of suffering, can never eradicate it. It is well to remember that although the prophecy at the end of the poem is for happiness,
there is no suggestion that Endymion's immortalization will
wipe away the painful aspects of his subjects' lives. He is a
prince, and in "Sleep and Poetry" Keats tells us that "they
shall be accounted poet kings / Who simply tell the most
heart-easing things" (lines 267–68). If the conclusion of
Endymion offers the prospect of everyone living happily
ever after, it is a happiness that must accommodate suffering, for that is the only happiness that is possible for hu-

mans. The wood through which Peona makes her way home is still a "gloomy" one, but she has been touched with "wonderment" (4. 1003), and that has made all the difference.

What, then, is the significance of Endymion's being immortalized at the end of the poem? Given even the slackest adherence to the mythical structure in which he is working, Keats can hardly avoid having Endymion "ensky'd" at the end if the poem is truly to be, as he called it, a "romance." But most readers have been dissatisfied with the poem's ending, and I share with them the opinion that Keats was not very pleased with it either.

After Endymion has chosen his earthly lover over his heavenly one but before he has been made aware of the final identity of the two, Keats interrupts his narrative:

> Endymion! unhappy! it nigh grieves
> Me to behold thee thus in last extreme:
> Ensky'd ere this, but truly that I deem
> Truth the best music in a first-born song.
> Thy lute-voic'd brother will I sing ere long,
> And thou shalt aid—hast thou not aided me?
> Yes, moonlight Emperor! felicity
> Has been thy meed for many thousand years;
> Yet often have I, on the brink of tears,
> Mourn'd as if yet thou wert a forester;—
> Forgetting the old tale.   (4. 770–80)

It seems to me an extreme misreading to interpret these lines, as Glen O. Allen and Stuart Sperry do, as a reflection of a change which takes place during the composition of the poem in Keats's attitude towards visionary experience.[25] I have already argued that Keats never believed that the insights of the imagination could be trusted as providing any reliable vision into the nature of ultimate reality. It is not Keats's attitude towards visionary experience that changes in this poem, but Endymion's. Endymion's eventual discovery that it is an illusion is the very lesson that his ordeal is meant to dramatize, for he must and does learn it on the pulses.

The anxiety revealed in these lines is of a wholly different kind. It has to do, I think, with the special problems posed by romance for a poet whose vision, as he indicates in "Sleep and Poetry," is essentially tragic. One is reminded of *Endymion*'s epigraph and its allusion to Shakespeare's sonnet, which is concerned with the question of credibility. Keats is concerned here with the whole issue of "truth" raised by the enskying of a mortal. "The age to come," says Shakespeare in that sonnet, "would say, 'This poet lies, / Such heavenly touches ne'er touched earthly faces.'" Keats is especially bothered by the prospect of immortalizing Endymion in his own poem, because he even finds it difficult to believe that Endymion was actually "ensky'd" in the old myth. "Forgetting the old tale," he keeps imagining that Endymion "yet . . . wert a forester." He imagines, that is to say, a tragic and not a romantic ending, for when he thinks of Endymion as still but a mortal, he does so "on the brink of tears," mourning Endymion's failure to be translated to heaven.

The reason, then, that Keats was dissatisfied with the ending of the poem has to do with his sense that he had not really solved the problem, inherent in a tragic view of life, of writing romance. We have only to turn to "The Eve of St. Agnes" to see the enormous progress Keats eventually made in dealing with this difficulty. We have already seen how, in that poem, he solves the problem of romance by embedding it in the larger context of tragedy. In *Endymion* too the consciousness of inevitable suffering is present, as the very first lines of the poem indicate; but in *Endymion* Keats did not, I think, find a narrative solution, since the happy ending necessitated by romance required that Endymion finally be immortalized. If there is a tension in the poem, it does not reflect any wavering on Keats's behalf about the essential issue of the allegory, for it is clear that the values attached to ideal beauty, immortality, and the heavenly realm are not finally in tension with, but are transferred to, the realm of earthly reality, mortality, and real, human beauty. But one cannot explain away the nagging fact that such a view does not find appropriate expression in the narrative device of immortalizing a mortal, and Keats more than anyone seems to have realized this fact.

The problem can be clarified by comparing the ending of *Endymion* with what we have of "Hyperion," a poem which Keats came clearly to see, during the composition of *Endymion*, would be an advance. In "Hyperion," instead of having a human made godlike through immortalization, a god (Apollo) becomes human through the paradoxical process of dying into mortality. In both instances Keats has the same point in mind: the spiritualization of the human. In *Endymion*, however, where the allegory is at such pains to demonstrate that the heavenly, immortal realm is a fiction, enskying Endymion at the end of the poem is a rather confusing way of embodying the metaphorical point in the allegorical structure. For even though it may be true that Keats intends the enskying of Endymion to represent the spiritualization of the human, the fact that the poem ends with Endymion moving beyond the human realm suggests an emphasis that seems quite at odds with the central emphasis of the allegory as I have interpreted it.

Keats seems to have found a more appropriate narrative solution in "Hyperion." In that poem he represents the secularizing process by having Apollo become human, but he also spiritualizes the secular by suggesting that the very act of assuming and intensely embracing humanity is what actually deifies Apollo in this new humanized religion, since the only true gods, like Psyche, reside in the human breast.

Keats's intention, I repeat, is the same as it is in *Endymion:* to spiritualize the human. But in "Hyperion" the technique of displacing the divine with the human and spiritualizing the latter does not clash with or obscure that central point. Even so, it cannot be overemphasized that the problem in *Endymion* originates not in a wavering conviction on the part of Keats but in the differing technical demands of romance and tragedy, in the sense in which I have been using those terms.[26]

In the lines from *Endymion* where Keats expresses his reservations about enskying Endymion, Keats seems to be aware of precisely this problem:

> Ensky'd ere this, but truly that I deem
> Truth the best music in a first-born song.
> Thy lute-voic'd brother will I sing ere long,
> And thou shalt aid—hast thou not aided me?
> Yes, moonlight Emperor!   (4. 772–76)

The "lute-voic'd brother" is of course Apollo, who will be the hero of "Hyperion." Keats thus distinguishes two types of poetry and acknowledges that although he must begin with the former, he will eventually move to the latter. The rather neat distinction between the moon and the sun tends to make these poems symbolic of the two poetic modes that Keats had distinguished in "Sleep and Poetry": that of "Flora, and old Pan" and that of "the agonies, the strife / Of human hearts." If Diana is, for Keats, the goddess of romance and Apollo the god of tragedy, then the moon becomes a symbol of romance and the sun becomes a symbol of tragedy.

Keats seems to be extremely self-conscious about this kind of distinction, for he makes it again in "On Sitting Down to Read King Lear Once Again," which was written in January 1818 while he was revising *Endymion* for the press. The

"golden tongued Romance" (line 1) to which he bids fare-
well is *Endymion*, which was, we remember, subtitled "A
Poetic Romance":

> Adieu! for, once again, the fierce dispute
> Betwixt damnation and impassion'd clay
> Must I burn through; once more humbly assay
> The bitter-sweet of this Shakespearian fruit.
>
> (lines 5–8)

He must leave behind his revision of a romance *(Endymion)*
for the reading of a tragedy *(King Lear)*, which he hopes will
inspire him to write his own tragedy:

> When through the old oak Forest I am gone,
> Let me not wander in a barren dream,
> But, when I am consumed in the fire
> Give me new Phoenix wings to fly at my desire.
>
> (lines 11–14)

Keats hopes that after he has completed his sojourn in "the
old oak Forest" of romance, he will have the power to write
true tragedy, the kind Shakespeare wrote.[27]

The tragedy he has in mind is "Hyperion," a poem that
itself contains more than a few allusions to *King Lear*. Keats
had already been contemplating "Hyperion" for four months
when he wrote this sonnet, and he refers directly to it in a
letter to Haydon written on the same day that he composed
the sonnet: "in Endymion I think you may have many bits
of the deep and sentimental cast—the nature of *Hyperion*
will lead me to treat it in a more naked and grecian Manner" (*Letters*, 1:207).

It is no surprise, then, that Keats's next major effort after
Endymion was "Hyperion." He had devoted one long poem
to romance, and he now turned to tragedy. The only surprise is that he did so before he had completed his self-
imposed ten-year apprenticeship. But Keats's estimate of the
number of years he would have to spend in the realm of
Flora and old Pan was quite exaggerated; the real signifi-

cance of his modesty about being prepared to write about the agony and strife of human hearts is that it indicates his own sense of inexperience and his own demanding standards. It is exactly this sentiment that Keats tells his brothers he was trying to illustrate in his new sonnet, "On Sitting Down to Read King Lear Once Again": "Nothing is finer for the purposes of great productions, than a very gradual ripening of the intellectual powers" (*Letters*, 1:214).

Nearly a year and a half later, in June 1819, Keats makes the same point still again. After contrasting "a noble Poet of Romance" with "a miserable and mighty Poet of the human Heart," he tells Miss Jeffrey: "I hope I am a little more of a Philosopher than I was, consequently a little less of a versifying Pet-lamb" (*Letters*, 2:115–16). The fact that these later distinctions are so consistent with the one Keats makes in "Sleep and Poetry" should give pause to those critics who deny that Keats knew very early the nature and direction of his poetic program and that he stuck to it without essentially altering it. From the very beginning, in fact, Keats's poetry had been infused with the knowledge of tragedy. The Pet-lamb in him had always had its deepest foundations in his own flint and iron.

IV

Keats's Historicism

Throughout his career Keats was preoccupied with the possibility of writing poetry that would represent a genuine advance over the monuments of the past. Constantly and doggedly, he measured his own achievements and goals against those of the great poets who had preceded him.[1] In the long letter to Reynolds written in May 1818, Keats takes up the subject directly, in the famous comparison of Milton and Wordsworth and in the simile of the "Mansion of Many Apartments." The whole letter is written with the same marvelous combination of playful irony and intense solemnity that characterizes the "vale of Soul-making" and the "finer tone" letters. In these, as in so many of his most famous speculations, Keats gracefully oscillates between buoyant frivolity and urgent seriousness. The tone of these letters is important, for its subtle blend of modesty and self-confidence is intimately related to Keats's sense of both the limitations and the glorious possibilities of life and poetry.

The yardstick that Keats uses to measure himself against Milton and Wordsworth, and to compare those two poets, is humanity. He wonders, for example, "whether Miltons apparently less anxiety for Humanity proceeds from his seeing further or no than Wordsworth: And whether Wordsworth . . . martyrs himself to the human heart, the main region [as Keats had learned and misquoted from the preface to *The Excursion*] of his song" (*Letters*, 1:278–79). Keats's transition to the "Mansion of Many Apartments" passage thus informs Reynolds that he will develop a "simile of human life as far as I now perceive it" in order "to show you how tall I stand by the giant [Wordsworth]" (*Letters*, 1:280). The elaborate simile which Keats then proceeds to develop again points up the importance of the historical context of Keats's "vast idea," for he viewed his new conception of life and poetry as a direct response to the problem of suffering in an age of increasing skepticism.

The comparison of Wordsworth with Milton occurs in a context that is decidedly relativistic in its tendency to attribute Wordsworth's superiority as an explorer of the human heart to "the general and gregarious advance of intellect, [rather] than individual greatness of Mind" (*Letters*, 1:281). Keats accounts for the fact that Milton "did not think [as deeply] into the human heart, as Wordsworth has done" (*Letters*, 1:282) by pleading the contingencies of Milton's historical period, for "in his time englishmen were just emancipated from a great superstition—and Men had got hold of certain points and resting places in reasoning which were too newly born to be doubted, and too much opposed by the Mass of Europe not to be thought etherial and authentically divine" (*Letters*, 1:281). Keats considers Milton's example proof that "there is really a grand march of intellect—, It proves that a mighty providence subdues the mightiest Minds to the service of the time being, whether it be in human Knowledge or Religion" (*Letters*, 1:282).

We need to pause a moment here and wonder why, if there is any truth in my argument, Keats relies on the notion of a "mighty providence" to explain why Wordsworth's understanding of the human heart "is deeper than Milton['s]." For *providence* seems to imply the very conception of divine intervention or control of human affairs that I have been suggesting Keats doubted. But the apparent contradiction is dissolved as soon as we realize that Keats's use of *providence* here is simply another example of his favorite technique of appropriating traditional religious terms to his own humanized religion.

Keats alerts us to this possibility by subtly altering the

significance of the larger simile which provides the context for this section of the letter. Critics have long recognized that the simile of "a large Mansion of Many Apartments" is based on John 14:1–3, where Christ explains to the Apostles: "Let not your heart be troubled: ye believe in God, believe also in me. In my Father's house are many mansions: if it were not so, I would have told you. I go to prepare a place for you. And if I go and prepare a place for you, I will come again, and receive you unto myself; that where I am, there ye may be also."[2]

The striking difference between Keats's and John's version of the simile is that in the biblical account the house is God's and it is divine life to which it is compared, whereas in Keats's version the house is the human heart and it is human life to which it is compared: "I compare human life to a large Mansion of Many Apartments" (*Letters*, 1:280). The alteration is crucial, for in the biblical version the house is located beyond temporal life, in heaven, whereas in Keats's it is located within temporal life, on earth, in human history.[3] In his characteristic fashion Keats has transposed the source of spirituality from the timeless or divine world to the temporal or human. As a result, his continued use of Christian terminology in the rest of the letter should be interpreted as performing this same non-Christian and radically humanized function.

What Keats means by *providence*, then, is not divine intervention in human history, but the very process of human history itself. Although he scorned all notions of human perfectibility and simplistic theories of progress, Keats did believe that the course of history involved a movement away from belief in higher reality and towards more human-centered forms of belief. The important point is that the "mighty providence," or the process of history, is itself the "grand march of intellect" to which Keats refers, since the direction of history's march is towards progressive humanization.[4]

It is in this kind of historical framework, then, that Keats conceives and locates his vast idea. If Wordsworth went beyond Milton as an explorer of the human heart, Keats, in keeping with the "grand march of intellect," would have to go beyond Wordsworth. In place of Milton's biblical revelation Wordsworth offered, explicitly in the preface to *The Excursion*, his own new revelation, a poetic version of the marriage of mind and nature which he thought surpassed the revelation of Milton:

> All strength—all terror, single or in bands,
> That ever was put forth in personal form—
> Jehovah—with his thunder, and the choir
> Of shouting Angels, and the empyreal thrones—
> I pass them unalarmed.
>
> . . . .
>
> How exquisitely the individual Mind
> (And the progressive powers perhaps no less
> Of the whole species) to the external World
> Is fitted:—and how exquisitely, too—
> Theme this but little heard of among men—
> The external World is fitted to the Mind.
>
> (lines 31–35, 63–68)

Keats saw clearly that Wordsworth was seeking new terms to describe the relationship of the human and divine, and he recognized that Wordsworth's solution to the problem represented a genuine advance in the direction of humanization. But Keats also seems to have realized that in another, perhaps more important, respect, Wordsworth shared more with Milton than he did with Keats himself. For all his secularization, Wordsworth still was engaged in an attempt to understand and explain the scheme by which the higher and quotidian realms were related. With Emerson he might have said that "things near are not less beautiful and wondrous than things remote. The near explains the far."[5] But so long as "the far" remained part of the equation, Keats could not embrace it.

If we conceive the "grand march of intellect" as an historical process of religious or spiritual humanization, Keats's advance over Wordsworth must be seen not as a quantitative advance but as a qualitative leap. For Keats has sliced the spiritual arena in half. He has not simply placed more emphasis on the human but, by removing the sphere of higher reality altogether and positing earthly reality as absolute, he has redirected spiritual aspiration and hope to this world. To restrict the spiritual arena to the human is not, however, to reduce the possibilities for spiritual fulfillment; on the contrary, it is to increase them, since for Keats the human realm discloses its rich spiritual possibilities only to those who have recognized the illusion of seeking fulfillment in some higher sphere and have opened themselves with intensity to this world.

By thus removing all external sanctions, Keats commits himself to a religion whose humanized character he laconically adumbrates in the "third Chamber of Life" (*Letters*, 1:282). Significantly, this third chamber is "stored with the wine of love—and the Bread of Friendship" (*Letters*, 1:283). Here again, Keats boldly appropriates the biblical and sacramental associations to his own religion, thus endowing many of the daily activities and relationships of human life with a sacramental character.

For Wordsworth, one can perceive the beauty of all things only after one has perceived the union of mind and nature—only, in other words, after one has grasped the larger scheme by which the things of this world are related to some larger realm that both includes and transcends the earthly. It is this larger reality that is the source of consolation, for it is because of their relation with this larger reality that the things of this world are holy. "All gratulant," says

Wordsworth near the end of *The Prelude,* "if rightly understood" (14. 387). But for Keats, who denies that transcendent
realm, beauty originates in the intensification of the human,
and the beautiful is holy not by virtue of its relation to any
larger context but because it consoles men and because it
enhances life and binds us to the earth.

Keats's religion requires no metaphysical foundation, and
he seems to be conscious of this fact when, just after telling
Reynolds about the "grand march of intellect" and the
"mighty providence," he apologizes for sounding so tedious:
"I have often pitied a Tutor who has to hear 'Nom^e: Musa'
—so often dinn'd into his ears—I hope you may not have
the same pain in this scribbling—I may have read these
things before, but I never had even a thus dim perception
of them; and moreover I like to say my lesson to one who
will endure my tediousness for my own sake—After all there
is certainly something real in the World" (*Letters,* 1:282).
The jocular, self-mocking tone is characteristic of Keats at
such moments, and it suggests, I think, his aversion to sys-
tematizing his speculations and his refusal to elevate them
to a metaphysical status. His use of the word *real* is significant in this regard; it has the force of giving validity to
human truths in the absence of metaphysical certainty. Keats
believes that his "dim perception" is not spurious, that it has
genuine human significance, but he refuses to posit it as
metaphysical truth. Instead, like Wordsworth and Milton
before him, he has been put "to the service of the time
being, whether it be in human Knowledge or Religion," and
the need of the present, as Keats conceives it, has been to
develop just such an alternative to traditional religion as he
has done here.

Keats thus found within the process of history itself the
standard against which all else must be measured, that is,

the development towards humanization. And it is that very standard against which he measures the poetic achievements of Milton, Wordsworth, and himself. The term *historicism* has been used in so many diverse ways that, like *romanticism,* its use is always problematic. But Maurice Mandelbaum provides a useful definition: *"Historicism is the belief that an adequate understanding of the nature of any phenomenon and an adequate assessment of its value are to be gained through considering it in terms of the place which it occupied and the role which it played within a process of development. . . .* What is, then, essential to historicism is the contention that a meaningful interpretation or adequate evaluation of any historical event involves seeing it as part of a stream of history."[6] Mandelbaum argues that although the Enlightenment conception of history differs from that of historicism, the Enlightenment did lay the groundwork for the development of historicism by extending the growth and range of interest in history and by emphasizing the doctrine of progress. I would suggest that while Keats shares a great deal with both the Enlightenment and the historicist conceptions of history as Mandelbaum characterizes them, Keats ultimately goes beyond them both.

For all the important differences between Keats and the thinkers of the Enlightenment, there are a number of striking similarities. In the first place, Keats shared Voltaire's belief that superstition must be overcome by enlightenment, that a new age was being born in which men would be generally freer from illusion than they had been in the past. Second, he believed that human history was a process that had no outside source, and he thus shared with the Enlightenment the progressivist view that history "proceeded according to a principle immanent within it" rather than transcending it. As such he stood in direct opposition to the Christian view that the reason for human history "was to be found in a state which lay outside of history." And finally, Keats believed "that there was a universally valid standard for the assessment of human achievements."[7] But while Keats did not deny that such a standard was accessible to reason, he did not place the kind of extreme trust in reason that Voltaire did. For Enlightenment thinkers like Voltaire the standard was arrived at through reason, whereas for Keats the standard was found within the very process of history itself, which he believed demonstrated a pattern of movement in a particular direction.

It is on the basis of this kind of historicism that Keats explains Wordsworth's advance over Milton yet avoids attributing it to "individual greatness of mind." Both poets' achievements are decisively influenced by their historical situations; if Wordsworth saw further into the human heart than Milton, that is because there is a constant historical movement in that direction. I say "decisively influenced" rather than "determined and bounded" because Keats's historicism stops short of the more extreme variety, which asserts not merely that historical factors greatly influence human thought, but that they actually determine it, and that every person is thus bounded by his inevitable historicity.

Keats is not so deterministic. As he begins the comparison of his two great predecessors, he confesses to Reynolds "an uncertainty whether Miltons apparently less anxiety for Humanity proceeds from his seeing further or no than Wordsworth" (*Letters*, 1:278). Keats goes on to argue that, at least on the basis of their poetry, Wordsworth seems to have seen further into the human heart than Milton. And it is what actually finds its way into the poetry that Keats is most concerned with in the comparison. But the fact that he acknowledges the possibility that Milton may actually have seen further than Wordsworth, even if his poetry does not reveal deeper human insights, is extremely significant. For

Keats seems to be assuming that it is possible to break out of one's historicity, to avoid the kind of historical determination that extreme historicists consider inevitable.

This is an extraordinarily thorny problem, and I do not wish to oversimplify it, or to conclude too readily that Keats's solution to it is paradoxical rather than contradictory. For on the face of it, Keats seems to be wanting it both ways. On the one hand he claims that human thought is decisively influenced by history and on the other that it need not be. The problem can be clarified, I think, by examining a letter that Keats wrote to Rice just six weeks earlier than the one we have been considering.

This is the letter in which Keats refers to Milton as "an active friend to Man." Just after that, he says:

> I must let you know that as there is ever the same quantity of matter constituting this habitable globe— as the ocean notwithstanding the enormous changes and revolutions taking place in some or other of its demesnes —notwithstanding Waterspouts whirlpools and mighty Rivers emptying themselves into it, it still is made ⟨of⟩ up of the same bulk—nor ever varies the number of its Atoms—And as a certain bulk of Water was instituted at the Creation—so very likely a certain portion of intellect was spun forth into the thin Air for the Brains of Man to prey upon it—You will see my drift without any unnecessary parenthesis. That which is contained in the Pacific and [read *can't?*] lie in the hollow of the Caspian—that which was in Miltons head could not find Room in Charles the seconds—he like a Moon attracted ⟨the⟩ Intellect to its flow—it has not ebbd yet— but has left the shore pebble all bare.   (*Letters*, 1:255)

It is not necessary to analyze the complex water imagery here to realize Keats's "drift," as he appropriately calls it. We are immediately struck by his repeated use of the word *intellect*, which is the same word he uses in the phrase "grand march of intellect" to refer to the human truth that history progressively discloses. What Keats is saying is that, just as the ocean goes through "enormous changes and revolutions" yet "still is made up of the same bulk," so too the history of human thought undergoes great changes yet still retains its essential truth: the development towards humanization.

Keats seems to be suggesting here that there is such a thing as absolute truth. But is not such a conception utterly at odds with the historicist's assumption that all truth is relative? To answer this question, we must first recall that for Keats the standard against which all else must be measured was to be found within the process of history itself, whereas the Enlightenment thinkers imposed upon history a universal standard which they deduced from the dictates of reason and took to be absolute truth. The historicist, on the other hand, while admitting the validity of finding a standard of measurement within the movement of history itself, has no way of dealing with a claim such as Keats's that the very process of history discloses a truth that does not transcend history but that is universal. The historicist assumes that a universal standard by which we can measure value depends on the validity of absolute or transhistorical truth, and since he denies the existence of absolute truth, he therefore denies the existence of universal standards of value and instead judges the value of any historical phenomenon only "in terms of its own inner harmony."[8] I have been insisting all along that Keats too denies the existence of transcendent truth, but the universal truth he finds in history is consistent with that position, for the universal truth is not itself transhistorical. It is, rather, human truth, the only truth we can know, and thus it is absolute truth.

Keats's very historicism, then, is what finally takes him beyond historicism. In fact, his whole conception of truth is meant to obviate the distinction between absolute and relative truth by substituting the idea of human truth, which is revealed in the very process of history. One is reminded, in this connection, of a similar point in the "Negative Capability" letter, in which Keats says that beauty not only "overcomes every other consideration" but that it "obliterates all [other] consideration." If this human truth is all we know on earth, it is also all we need to know.

I think we can understand now why Keats does not include Shakespeare in his comparison of himself with Milton and Wordsworth, whereas so often in his letters and poems he holds out Shakespeare as his highest model. Keats is considering the historical movement towards increased humanization, and Milton, Wordsworth, and Keats each represent successive steps in that direction. Shakespeare, quite simply, has already arrived. Nor does that fact contradict Keats's claim that the larger movement of history truly is becoming more humanized. By avoiding the more deterministic form of historicism, Keats can confidently and consistently assume that it is possible for Shakespeare to have understood human truth even though he lived at an earlier time. Although Keats's own age may be more enlightened than Shakespeare's, that does not mean that everyone in Keats's age will be free from illusion. Similarly, though the "grand march of intellect" may have made Keats's age more readily receptive to human truth, that is no reason why Shakespeare could not have perceived it as well. And as Keats's consistently superlative evaluations of Shakespeare make clear, Keats believed that Shakespeare did see the same human truth that he did.

The final and ultimately antihistoricist implication of these ideas of Keats is that the development of human thought can go no further than the knowledge of human truth. Keats seems to have recognized that such a conclusion was implicit in historicism itself, for the very conception of development, as Mandelbaum says, involves "the notion of goal-orientation."[9] If the history of human thought displays a discernible tendency towards humanization, it is inescapable that full humanization marks the end of that history's development. To say as much is to recite a tautology. The reason, then, that Keats was so excited about his vast idea was that he knew it was not merely an advance over the dominant ideas of the past, or a closer approximation to humanized truth, or a more consoling myth, but that it was as far as one could go, that it constituted an understanding of human truth that, conceived in these terms, could never be superseded. Nor was it a contradiction to preclude this truth from the historicist claim that all truth is relative, for it was on historicist grounds that Keats perceived the truth in the first place.

We are now in a position to understand still another crux in the long letter to Reynolds: the apparent contradiction between Keats's statement that he can only describe two of the chambers, and the fact that he does, near the end of the letter, describe the third chamber. If it is true, as Keats himself says, that the "doors of the rest" of the chambers beyond the second are "as yet shut upon me" (*Letters*, 1:280), how can he perceive the nature of the third? To answer this question, we must first remind ourselves that the simile of the mansion refers not just to the historical development of human thought but also to the development of each individual life. If the "vale of Soul-making" metaphor refers to the individual process of humanization, and the "grand march of intellect" to the historical process of it, the "Mansion of Many Apartments" simile refers to both. "It had been widely assumed," says Mandelbaum, "that the stages through which civilization passes must resemble the stages through which the individual passes in his development toward maturity. In biology, such an assumption seemed to have been more than an analogy, and to have been established as a fact through the evolutionary interpretation of embryology —a fact summarized in the doctrine that ontogeny recapitulates phylogeny." An earlier version of this view, popularized in the quarrel between the ancients and the moderns, suggested "that human history could be regarded as analogous to the development of an individual from infancy to maturity: in the early years there was a lack of the experience necessary for knowledge."[10]

It was exactly that sense of inexperience that led Keats to commit himself to a ten-year apprenticeship in the realm of Flora and old Pan. Nor can this connection be explained as a mere coincidence. On the contrary, it confirms our earlier assertion that the program for poetry that Keats outlined in "Sleep and Poetry" was based on precisely the same conception of life that characterized his mature insights. For the letter we have been examining assumes this very same connection between the program for poetry and both the historical and individual processes of humanization. That, after all, is the basis on which Keats measures himself against Milton and Wordsworth. We have already considered the connection between Keats's poetic program and the historical process of humanization; but to determine how Keats could perceive the nature of the third chamber when, by his own account, its doors were still shut, we must turn to the relationship between Keats's poetic program and the process of individual development.

Like the development of human thought in history, the concept of individual human development has a built-in teleology. Keats never tired of reminding himself that only through actual experience could he develop and confirm that human knowledge which above all he desired. He realized very early that this knowledge inevitably involved an understanding of the agony and the strife of the human heart. But although he already understood that that was the highest subject for poetry, he did not yet feel prepared to do it full justice, for he felt he lacked the necessary human experience.

Although he was already engaged in writing about the agonies of the human heart when he wrote this letter to Reynolds in May 1818, Keats still felt—to the very end, in fact—that he had a long way to go. "Now if we live," Keats tells Reynolds, "and go on thinking, we too [like Wordsworth] shall explore" the "dark Passages" beyond the second chamber (*Letters*, 1:281). As we learn from his brief characterization of the third chamber, Keats already has a sense of what it is like, just as, in "Sleep and Poetry," he knows that ultimately poetry must deal with human strife. But to know the goal is not to realize it in poetry.

What matters most for Keats is not simply knowing the goal, but being able to write the kind of poetry that actually reveals its beauty and truth. It is one thing to perceive the nature of the third chamber, but it is quite another to be able to express its distinctive color and texture and tone, to be able to convey its simple yet elusive profundity. Keats greatly admires Wordsworth's ability to embody and communicate his vision of things even if Wordsworth has not seen into the third chamber: "he is a Genius and superior [to] us, in so far as he can, more than we, make discoveries, and *shed a light in them*" (*Letters*, 1:281; emphasis mine). As the phrasing suggests, Keats is not saying here that Wordsworth has seen further than Keats has, but that he has more adequately illuminated what he has seen. Keats feels that his own poetry too must be judged on the basis of how successfully he illuminates his own vision of the third chamber. As he continues to grow in experience, Keats too will explore the dark passages more thoroughly, but that will take time. The important difference between him and Wordsworth is that although Keats does not yet feel adequate to describe and illuminate the third chamber, he does in fact see it; Wordsworth, for all his genius, has not seen the third chamber, so that his illuminations, brilliant as they are, remain fixed somewhere between the domain of Milton and the new religious and poetic territory staked out by Keats.

Once again we are at the heart of Keats's profoundly paradoxical sense of the limitations and possibilities of human life and poetry. It is no accident that critics with widely divergent views of Keats have at least agreed that there are two essential impulses in his work, the one constricting and the other extending human possibilities. But the fundamental consistency of those impulses, and the extraordinary spiritual integrity and power of mind that underlie them, can be understood only if we are willing to take Keats as seriously as I have been arguing we must. For Keats believed that he had discovered the foundation on which a new and permanent kind of religion and poetry could be based. That is why, in his first major poem, when he talks about poetry's function, he talks not about *a* function, but about *the* function: "the great end / Of poesy" and "the end and aim of Poesy" ("Sleep and Poetry," lines 245–46, 293). And that is also why, in one of his last major poems, he describes Moneta's temple as "that eternal domed monument," permanent amidst "the faulture of [such] decrepit things" as "grey Cathedrals" (*The Fall of Hyperion*, 1. 71, 70, 67).

If Shakespeare could surmount his historicity, it would also be possible for Keats to write romance that included an understanding of tragedy, since the movement of Keats's poetic program from romance to tragedy constitutes a parallel not only to the personal development of an individual suggested in the conception of soul-making, but also to the historical development of human thought suggested in the idea of the "grand march of intellect."[11] And Keats's romance did, in fact, demonstrate an understanding of tragedy. Even at this level of his speculations we find that same profound coherence. So far is Keats's work from demonstrating conflicting impulses that one wonders whether, varying

128

moods notwithstanding, a single important spiritual contradiction is to be found in his poems and letters.

⸻

The close connection between his conceptions of life and
poetry and the values according to which he apparently led
his own life has always been a major source of Keats's great
appeal. The interpretation that I have been offering should
not only confirm that connection but deepen its significance.
For the "third Chamber of Life," which is "stored with the
wine of love—and the Bread of Friendship," is where Keats
seems to have led his life. One thinks, for example, of the
extraordinary value he placed on friendship and close family
relations. It is important to keep this in mind when we hear
Keats telling us in "Ode on a Grecian Urn" that poetry is "a
friend to man" (line 48), or that Milton was "an active friend
to Man . . . and has been since his death" (*Letters*, 1:255).

The sprightly and devoted letters to his sister, the touch-
ing early sonnet "To My Brothers," the agony over and un-
failing loyalty to Tom, and the long and tender letters to
George and Georgiana in America—all of these reveal an
aspect of Keats's life that was inseparably related to his religious conception of poetry and of humanity. Even in his
relations with his family and friends we see a man largely
preoccupied with the personal problems of suffering and
death and continuously struggling to find consolation in the
beauty and warmth of close human relationships. "I have
Fanny and I have you," he tells George and Georgiana while
Tom is dying: "three people whose Happiness to me is
sacred— . . . the tears will come into your Eyes—let them—
and embrace each other—thank heaven for what happiness
you have and after thinking a moment or two that you
suffer in common with all Mankind hold it not a sin to re-
gain your cheerfulness" (*Letters*, 1:391–92). Comments like

this, which might otherwise be charged with the same kind of mawkish tender-mindedness that some critics attribute to Keats's aestheticism, can be understood in a new light once we realize that, like the aestheticism, the tender-mindedness really springs from an extraordinary tough-mindedness, and that beneath the Pet-lamb lies a solid bed of flint and iron.

One begins to see the paradox in Keats's attitude towards poetry's possibilities when one examines that attitude within this larger context of aestheticism as a solution to the problems posed by skepticism. There is, for example, a sense in which Keats regarded the poet as a kind of secular priest, but in a form radically different from Wordsworth's conception of the poet-priest. Whereas for Wordsworth the poet transfigures the harsh realities of the mundane world by mediating a vision of the union of mind and nature, for Keats such a transfiguration is neither possible nor desirable. Instead, the poet undertakes the neoreligious task of pursuing knowledge—*human* knowledge—and making it the foundation of a poetry that ministers to the human heart by consoling it with beauty. Keats reacts strongly against Wordsworth's conviction that poetry, acting as a kind of Scripture, has a special claim as a means of salvation. This reaction provides part of the force behind Keats's objection to the "egotistical sublime," and it is closely connected to Keats's occasional skepticism about the value of any poetry.

"I am sometimes so very sceptical," he tells Bailey, "as to think Poetry itself a mere Jack a lanthern to amuse whoever may chance to be struck with its brilliance—As Tradesmen say every thing is worth what it will fetch" (*Letters*, 1:242).[12] Keats put such a great premium on poetry that occasionally he wondered whether it could perform its high function of consolation adequately. But poetry was not the only means of consolation. Some people, Keats said, "do it with their society—some with their wit—some with their benevolence —some with a sort of power of conferring pleasure and good humour on all they meet" (*Letters*, 1:271). Yet for himself, Keats knows that "there is but one way" (*Letters*, 1:271): the writing of poetry.[13]

The pursuit of knowledge and the preparation to write the real poetry of the agony of the human heart preoccupied Keats throughout his short career. He was always conscious that his efforts were not enough and often fearful that he would never be able to glean from his "teeming brain" the "full-ripen'd grain."[14] Still, although he was forever preparing for the future and particularly for his great ambition to write plays, he did receive more than his fair share of exposure to suffering, and he gradually began to feel that he was making progress on the long journey from pastoral to tragedy. "I hope I am a little more of a Philosopher than I was," he writes in June 1819, "consequently a little less of a versifying Pet-lamb" (*Letters*, 2:116). "Philosopher" here has the same meaning that it does in "On Seeing a Lock of Milton's Hair": not metaphysician but one who has wisdom or knowledge of human life. In "Hyperion," to which we now turn, Keats insists again that the kind of human knowledge upon which a true religion of beauty can be based is deeply tragic.

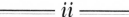

The allegory of "Hyperion" is twofold: it concerns the birth of a new kind of poetry and of a new kind of religion, which is the foundation of the new poetry. Both arise out of particular historical circumstances and human needs, and, like all poetry and religions for Keats, they are to be judged according to how successfully they satisfy those needs. For all the critical dispute about the dangers of interpreting Oceanus's position as Keats's own, it seems plain to me that Oceanus's view is quite consistent with Keats's position, as I have just outlined it, in regard to historicism. "We fall by

course of Nature's law," Oceanus tells the Titans, "not force /
Of thunder, or of Jove" (2. 181–82). In Keats's version of the
Fall, it is not a power beyond history that controls historical
development, but the very process of history itself. Oceanus
thus tells Saturn, king of the Titans:

> And first, as thou wast not the first of powers,
> So art thou not the last; it cannot be:
> Thou art not the beginning nor the end.
>
> . . . .
>
> So on our heels a fresh perfection treads,
> A power more strong in beauty, born of us
> And fated to excel us, as we pass
> In glory that old Darkness.
>
> (2. 188–90, 212–15)

What Oceanus is explaining here is the "grand march of
intellect," the process by which one view of the world gives
way to a newer, more humanistic one by virtue of an apparently natural law of historical change which "subdues the
mightiest Minds to the service of the time being." The fall
of the Titans and the rise of the Olympians thus represent
the decline of an outmoded religion and its replacement by
a religion that better meets the needs of the present. Notice
too that the new race is "more strong in beauty," an idea
that Oceanus formulates into a characteristic Keatsian principle: " 'tis the eternal law / That first in beauty should be
first in might" (2. 228–29). The "law" states not a metaphysical proposition but the human truth of beauty's great
power. For the law is based, Oceanus tells us, on "eternal
truth" (2. 187), which is revealed in the very process of history itself. Not surprisingly, in the lines that follow Oceanus
makes the connection with consolation. He came to his fellow Titans, he says:

> to see how dolorous fate
> Had wrought upon ye; and how I might best
> Give consolation in this woe extreme.

Receive the truth, and let it be your balm.

(2. 240–43)

If it seems peculiar to be talking about the way in which religions serve human needs in a poem whose characters are gods rather than humans, we need only remind ourselves that for Keats, all gods reside in the human breast, even if their originators do not acknowledge the fact. Therefore (and here Keats shares the view of Blake), the particular gods of a people will reflect that people's view of reality—providing, of course, that the people believe in the religion. Like all historical phenomena, religions arise out of the needs and values of their age. Keats can thus tell the story of the rise and fall of gods and at the same time, quite consistently, assume that it contains the story of human history. Keats is concerned in "Hyperion" to secularize the great themes of the Fall—innocence, knowledge, suffering—and to demonstrate in what ways it must be regarded as a fortunate Fall.

The new Olympian religion is not only more humanized than that of the Titans; it is also less innocent, and as such it represents an advance. For the Titans are indeed an innocent race, and they are baffled by this sudden intrusion of danger and destruction into their lives. "Why / Is my eternal essence thus distraught," Hyperion asks himself, "To see and to behold these horrors new?" (1. 231–33):

> Saturn is fallen, am I too to fall?
> Am I to leave this haven of my rest,
> This cradle of my glory, this soft clime,
> This calm luxuriance of blissful light,
> These crystalline pavilions, and pure fanes,
> Of all my lucent empire? (1. 234–39)

It is a marvelous innocence, like the "happy pieties" of the Greeks in "Ode to Psyche," and Keats looks nostalgically upon it; nonetheless, it is innocence based on illusion and

133

thus ill-equipped to deal with the harsh reality of suffering. As Enceladus says:

> The days of peace and slumberous calm are fled;
> Those days, all innocent of scathing war,
>
> . . . .
>
> .   .   .   before our brows were taught to frown.
> (2. 335–36, 339)

Oceanus's speech is meant to console the Titans with the balm of truth: "And in the proof much comfort will I give, / If ye will take that comfort in its truth" (2. 179–80). He realizes how difficult it is to take comfort in a painful truth, but he insists on the need to do so nonetheless:

> Now comes the pain of truth, to whom 'tis pain;
> O folly! for to bear all naked truths,
> And to envisage circumstance, all calm,
> That is the top of sovereignty. Mark well!
> (2. 202–5)

Oceanus understands that truth is painful and that the Titans must be consoled in their sorrow, but his explanation of the situation is too abstract, too impatient to make it as consoling as he had hoped it would be. Keats, while he shares Oceanus's assessment of the situation, demonstrates a more immediate and tolerant kind of sympathy:

> Then Thea spread abroad her trembling arms
> Upon the precincts of this nest of pain,
> And sidelong fix'd her eye on Saturn's face:
> There saw she direst strife; the supreme God
> At war with all the frailty of grief,
> Of rage, of fear, anxiety, revenge,
> Remorse, spleen, hope, but most of all despair.
> Against these plagues he strove in vain; for Fate
> Had pour'd a mortal oil upon his head,
> A disanointing poison: so that Thea,
> Affrighted, kept her still, and let him pass
> First onwards in, among the fallen tribe.
> (2. 89–100)

This is simply one of many examples of Keats's humanization of the Titans, and like the others it is meant to demonstrate that despite their illusions, these Titans genuinely are
feeling the agony of suffering. Keats's sympathetic imaginative grasp of their situation reminds us that though one may
be consoled for suffering its pain yet remains.

Oceanus's explanation of the forward movement of history
does not imply the acceptance of Godwinian perfectibility,
as some critics have suggested. When Oceanus says, "on our
heels a fresh perfection treads" (2. 212), he is suggesting not
that suffering will ultimately be eliminated but that each
new religion seems to represent a further step away from
illusion. But what is most striking about Oceanus's account
of the grand march of history is its extraordinary inclusive-
ness, embracing not just pagan religions but, by virtue of its
loaded imagery, the biblical religions as well:

> Thou art not the beginning nor the end.
> From Chaos and parental Darkness came
> Light.   (2. 190–92)

By thus embedding allusions to Revelation and Genesis
in a catalogue of other fallen religions, Keats denies Christianity the unique status it claims and implies that all religions must be viewed as human phenomena. Indeed, the
corridors of history are filled with dead religions. The Titans,
for example, are compared to the Druids. As they loiter in
their den, they resemble nothing so much as old religious
relics:

> Scarce images of life, one here, one there,
> Lay vast and edgeways; like a dismal cirque
> Of Druid stones, upon a forlorn moor.
>   (2. 33–35)

One is reminded of the induction to *The Fall of Hyperion*,
in which Keats, standing by an "old sanctuary" (1. 62), looks
down at a wasteland of religious remnants, the collective
detritus of the ages:

> Upon the marble at my feet there lay
> Store of strange vessels, and large draperies,
> Which needs had been of dyed asbestos wove,
> Or in that place the moth could not corrupt,
> So white the linen; so, in some, distinct
> Ran imageries from a sombre loom.
> All in a mingled heap confus'd there lay
> Robes, golden tongs, censer, and chafing dish,
> Girdles, and chains, and holy jewelries—.
>
> (1. 72–80)

These obsolete remains have the same status for Keats as

> grey Cathedrals, buttress'd walls, rent towers,
> The superannuations of sunk realms,
> Or Nature's Rocks toil'd hard in waves and winds.
>
> (1. 67–69)

They are all, in Keats's phrase, "decrepit things" (1. 70).

This concern with dead and dying religions and myths runs throughout "Hyperion." Near the beginning of book 3, for example, Keats says he must leave the Titans:

> Leave them, O Muse! for thou anon wilt find
> Many a fallen old Divinity
> Wandering in vain about bewildered shores.
>
> (3. 7–9)

And in book 1 we are told that lightning was considered a kind of

> hieroglyphics old
> Which sages and keen-eyed astrologers
> Then living on the earth, with labouring thought
> Won from the gaze of many centuries:
> Now lost, save what we find on remnants huge
> Of stone, or marble swart; their import gone,
> Their wisdom long since fled.   (1. 277–83)

Even after the "import" of a myth or religion is "gone" and its "wisdom long since fled," the myth itself remains, and although the most beautiful myth is that which has the most human truth, even outworn myths, devoid of their original significance, can be beautiful. That is one reason, of course, why Keats turns to Greek mythology in the first place. When the happy pieties of a religion lose their hold on a people, the lovely old legends and stories remain, like the "beautiful Tales which," Keats tells his sister, "have come down from the ancient times of that beautiful Greece" (*Letters*, 1:154). It is the myths themselves that die last.

If religions rise and fall according to changing human needs, there yet remains a principle of stability or permanence. When Hyperion finds himself incapable of making the sun rise again, Keats observes:

> Fain would he have commanded, fain took throne
> And bid the day begin, if but for change.
> He might not:—No, though a primeval God:
> The sacred seasons might not be disturb'd.
>
> (1. 290–93)

Though all else changes, nature remains the same. This recognition dawns on Hyperion with the force of a discovery so overwhelming that at first he can only stare blankly:

> Hyperion arose, and on the stars
> Lifted his curved lids, and kept them wide
> Until it ceas'd; and still he kept them wide:
> And still they were the same bright, patient stars.
>
> (1. 350–53)

One is simultaneously reminded of "Bright Star" and "On First Looking into Chapman's Homer," in which

> Cortez . . . with eagle eyes
> . . . star'd at the Pacific—and all his men
> Look'd at each other with a wild surmise—
> Silent, upon a peak in Darien.   (lines 11–14)

But a more important parallel is "To Autumn," in which Keats recognizes that nature resembles the human condition in its changes of season but significantly differs in its unceasing cycles of death and rebirth. The crucial difference

between Keats's position in "To Autumn" and Hyperion's
position in these lines is that whereas Keats accepts and
even embraces the human condition that inevitably involves
change, Hyperion can only recoil from it. Consequently,
after finally realizing what he is up against, Hyperion goes
off in search of Saturn, leaping into the oblivion of the
night:

> Like to a diver in the pearly seas,
> Forward he stoop'd over the airy shore,
> And plung'd all noiseless into the deep night.
> (1. 355–57)

Hyperion finds it impossible to conceive that nature could
remain the same while he has changed. He cannot comprehend the human truth that underlies both this poem and
"To Autumn": that nature survives all our interpretations of
it. Wallace Stevens is driving at a similar point in his extremely Keatsian "Sunday Morning":

> There is not any haunt of prophecy,
> Nor any old chimera of the grave,
> Neither the golden underground, nor isle
> Melodious, where spirits gat them home,
> Nor visionary south, nor cloudy palm
> Remote on heaven's hill, that has endured
> As April's green endures; or will endure
> Like her remembrance of awakened birds,
> Or her desire for June and evening, tipped
> By the consummation of the swallow's wings.
> (lines 51–60)

The knowledge that Hyperion lacks is precisely the
knowledge that Apollo, like Keats, passionately seeks and
eventually discovers. But only in the profound silence of
Mnemosyne's face can the "wondrous lesson" be "read" (3.
111–12), by a supreme act of Negative Capability, figured in
Keats's familiar image of the silent gaze:

> [Apollo's] enkindled eyes, with level glance
> Beneath his white soft temples, stedfast kept

Trembling with light upon Mnemosyne.
(3. 121–23)

The "pain of truth" that Apollo learns is Keats's ideal of "disinterestedness" (*Letters*, 2:79):

> to bear all naked truths,
> And to envisage circumstance, all calm,
> That is the top of sovereignty. (2. 203–5)

The ideal is based on the need to come to grips with suffering, and in one of his letters describing "disinterestedness" Keats uses the plural form of the same word, *circumstance*, in this very connection: "Circumstances are like Clouds continually gathering and bursting—While we are laughing the seed of some trouble is put into the wide arable land of events" (*Letters*, 2:79). What Apollo learns, then, is that tragedy is the deepest human truth, and that it is also, paradoxically, the most beautiful: "How beautiful, if sorrow had not made / Sorrow more beautiful than Beauty's self" (1. 35–36).

The new Olympian religion being born is based on exactly this conception of human truth and beauty. But of course it is not Keats's purpose to characterize the actual historical phenomenon of Olympian religion as such. As "Ode to Psyche" and "Ode on a Grecian Urn" make clear, Keats considered that old Greek religion decidedly more innocent than his own, even if it was less innocent than that of the Titans. Keats simply uses the Olympians in "Hyperion" to represent a new religion that is both less innocent and more humanized than the one it replaces. The allegorical implication is that, just as the Olympians superseded the Titans, Keats's new religion will replace Christianity. For not only, Oceanus says, is it natural that the Olympians have displaced the Titans, but "Yea, by that [same] law, another race may drive / Our conquerors to mourn as we do now" (2. 230–31). Although allegorically the Olympians represent

Keats's religion, historically they are but one earlier stage in a developmental process that is completed only in Keats's own religion.

It should already be clear that Keats has not involved himself in a contradiction by allowing Oceanus to grasp "eternal truth" even though he belongs to a race that Keats himself tells us is filled with illusion. Difficult as it may be to see beyond the general conceptual horizon of one's own age, it is not impossible, as Shakespeare's example conclusively demonstrates for Keats. Nor is Keats himself, in his own actual historical situation, entirely free from the necessity to see beyond his time. Although skepticism had become more than a little common in the post-Enlightenment period, it could scarcely be said that Christianity had utterly lost its hold on people; indeed, during Keats's lifetime evangelical movements were increasing their successes. But if Christianity was not yet in its death throes, it at least occupied a less secure position than it had a few centuries earlier, and for Keats, in any case, a new religion was in the process of being born. The fall of the Titans and the rise of the Olympians were above all meant to dramatize the decline of Christianity and the emergence of Keats's humanized religion.

It is in this context that the relationship of "Hyperion" to Milton's "Nativity" ode becomes clear. We remember that in "Ode to Psyche" it is Keats himself who creates for Psyche the religious perquisites and paraphernalia normally attached to a goddess. Before he comes along she has none:

> temple thou hast none,
> Nor altar heap'd with flowers;
> Nor virgin-choir to make delicious moan
> Upon the midnight hours;
> No voice, no lute, no pipe, no incense sweet
> From chain-swung censer teeming;
> No shrine, no grove, no oracle, no heat

Of pale-mouth'd prophet dreaming.
                                        (lines 28–35)

Some editors and critics have noted that these lines recall
Milton's "On the Morning of Christ's Nativity"; but no one,
to my knowledge, has adequately explained the significance
of this extremely important allusion. Keats's allusion to Milton's celebration of the infant Christ's victory over the
pagan gods establishes a parallel between Christianity's displacement of paganism and the implicit displacement of
Christianity by Keats's new religion. In the "Nativity" ode
it is Apollo who has become ineffectual because of the coming of Christ:

> The Oracles are dumb,
> No voice or hideous hum
>   Runs through the arched roof in words deceiving.
> *Apollo* from his shrine
> Can no more divine,
>   With hollow shriek the steep of *Delphos* leaving.
> No nightly trance, or breathed spell,
> Inspires the pale-ey'd Priest from the prophetic cell.
>   (lines 173–80)

In "Ode to Psyche" Keats declares himself a new prophet-
priest in language that recalls Milton's description of Apollo:

> So let me be thy choir, and make a moan
>   Upon the midnight hours;
> Thy voice, thy lute, thy pipe, thy incense sweet
>   From swinged censer teeming;
> Thy shrine, thy grove, thy oracle, thy heat
>   Of pale-mouth'd prophet dreaming.
>   (lines 44–49)

The procedure is similar to that of "Hyperion": by identifying with Apollo Keats humanizes the god of poetry and thus
revitalizes him for a post-Christian world.[15]

In the "Nativity" ode Milton equates the coming of the
dawn, the rising of the *sun,* with the coming of Christ, the
son. In a familiar image Christ is identified with light. In

"Hyperion" Keats calls attention to this connection by emphasizing Hyperion's and Apollo's association with light. Hyperion is first introduced as "Blazing Hyperion [sitting] on his orbed fire" (1. 166). "His flaming robes stream'd out beyond his heels" (1. 214), and Enceladus describes him as "his radiance" (2. 345). Later we are told that "a splendour" appeared (2. 357), and all of nature "now saw the light and made it terrible. / It was Hyperion" (2. 366–67). Keats often describes Apollo as "golden" and "bright," and in a central image near the end of the poem he drives home the light imagery:

> Thus the God,
> While his enkindled eyes, with level glance
> Beneath his white soft temples, stedfast kept
> Trembling with light upon Mnemosyne.
> (3. 120–23)

The function of these images is to throw into relief the parallel between Hyperion, Apollo, and Christ that is implicit in the fact that all three are associated with the sun.

But there is a more important comparison between Christ and Apollo. At the end of the poem, when Apollo "die[s] into life" (3. 130), one is of course reminded of Christ's incarnation. The difference is that while Christ becomes human only after being a god, Apollo becomes a Keatsian god only by first becoming human. Apollo can be deified in the new religion only after he has opened himself to the painful but beautiful knowledge of the human:

> Knowledge enormous makes a God of me.
> Names, deeds, gray legends, dire events, rebellions,
> Majesties, sovran voices, agonies,
> Creations and destroyings, all at once
> Pour into the wide hollows of my brain,
> And deify me, as if some blithe wine
> Or bright elixir peerless I had drunk,
> And so become immortal.   (3. 113–20)

Like Christ, Apollo assumes the burden of mortality, but unlike Christ, his deity is contingent on his humanity. Yet it is important that we understand the nature of Apollo's divinity. Like all gods, he exists only in the human breast, but that fact is now openly acknowledged by his Keatsian worshippers, whose realization that he is an intensity of their own making distinguishes Apollo from Christ, whose worshippers claim that he also exists beyond the human realm. Apollo does not transcend human history; he lives only within it, and serves only its needs. His immortality and divinity are thus metaphors for the intensity of his humanity and for the life-affirming power of beauty which that intensity reveals.

Apollo, we remember, is not just the god of poetry but also the god of healing. Gittings is right to remind us of the similar situation of Keats, who was himself both doctor and poet,[16] and the parallel lends all the more significance to Keats's conception, in *The Fall of Hyperion,* of the poet as "humanist, Physician to all men" (1. 190). The crucial implication of the relationship between poet and healer is precisely that conception of poetry as consolation that Keats celebrated in "Sleep and Poetry": "to sooth the cares, and lift the thoughts of man" (line 247). In that early poem Keats said that although he did not yet feel ready to write the poetry of "the agonies, the strife / Of human hearts," he knew that such tragic poetry was the most consoling, because the most beautiful, kind. Now, in both "Hyperion" and *The Fall of Hyperion,* he reasserts that belief by basing the new Apollonian poetry on the new humanized religion of beauty.

In their inclusion of sorrow and pain the beautiful songs of Apollo seem to answer a newly felt need, which is illustrated in the Titan Clymene. Clymene had come to a shore, she tells us, where she sought some comfort for her grief.

But the natural surroundings seemed out of joint with her feelings:

> I stood upon a shore, a pleasant shore,
> Where a sweet clime was breathed from a land
> Of fragrance, quietness, and trees, and flowers.
> Full of calm joy it was, as I of grief;
> Too full of joy and soft delicious warmth;
> So that I felt a movement in my heart
> To chide, and to reproach that solitude
> With songs of misery, music of our woes.
>
> (2. 262–69)

I take this landscape as symbolic of the whole innocent world of the Titans, which can provide no adequate basis for consolation. And it is precisely because it is so innocent, and thus cannot offer satisfactory consolation, that the world of the Titans is on the verge of death. In its place, as Clymene dimly senses here, must come a religion that can deal with suffering without escaping from it or explaining it away.

The melodies that then drift towards Clymene are the songs of that new religion which is just now entering the world, and they displace her own noble but inadequate "songs of misery" just as the new religion will replace hers. Clymene recognizes the tragic character of this new poetry, and she senses its beauty and power. "There came an enchantment," she says, "that did both drown and keep alive my ears" (2. 276–77). "My sense was fill'd," she says,

> With that new blissful golden melody.
> A living death was in each gush of sounds.
>
> (2. 279–81)

Finally, overcome with grief, she covers her ears, but

> past all hindrance of my trembling hands,
> A voice came sweeter, sweeter than all tune,
> And still it cried, "Apollo! young Apollo!

The morning-bright Apollo! young Apollo!"
                                    (2. 291–94)

Though she responds to the new poetry passionately, she cannot accept the strange combination "of joy and grief at once" (2. 289) that it makes her feel. She has moved beyond the entrance of the "Chamber of Maiden-Thought," that point of spiritual development in which "we become intoxicated with the light and the atmosphere, we see nothing but pleasant wonders, and think of delaying there for ever in delight." But she is stalled in this chamber, at the point of discovering "that the World is full of Misery and Heartbreak" (*Letters*, 1:281). "All my knowledge," she tells Saturn,

> is that joy is gone,
> And this thing woe crept in among our hearts,
> There to remain for ever, as I fear.   (2. 253–55)

Clymene cannot see beyond the second chamber, for she has been overwhelmed by the vision of suffering, and her dim perception of its beauty fades into insignificance in the face of the crushing loss of innocence which engulfs her. The "knowledge enormous [which] makes a God" of Apollo is Keats's version of the Fortunate Fall: far from restricting one's chances for happiness, the loss of innocence increases them, for it makes possible a perception of beauty in suffering, as Apollo's songs demonstrate. But just as the Titanic religion provides Hyperion no context in which to understand change, it provides Clymene no means of comprehending suffering. She concludes, therefore, that her experience has made her realize "that we [Titans] had parted from all hope" (2. 261).

Clymene can be consoled by neither the truths of Oceanus nor the bittersweet songs of Apollo. One can understand how, for all its truth, Oceanus's speech would yet lack the

power to console. Although it is not a cold-blooded or re-
pugnantly aloof speech, neither does it convey the kind of
sympathetic understanding that we find in Keats's treatment
of the Titans. Apollo's songs surely reveal the beauty of
painful truth more successfully than Oceanus's speech, and
the fact that Clymene is not finally consoled by them tells
us more about the limitations of her culture and her own
spiritual development than about any failings in Apollo's
poetry.

I have applied the terms of the "Mansion of Many Apartments" letter to Clymene's experience because the simile of
human life in that letter, like the allegory in "Hyperion,"
applies not only to the historical movement of religion and
poetry but also to the spiritual development of individuals.
The Titanic view of reality that structures Hyperion's and
Clymene's consciousness denies them the life-affirming perception that process is the law of life and that change must
be embraced and celebrated, as Keats celebrates it, for
example, in "To Autumn" or "Ode on Melancholy." Only
when one sees the "eternal truth" that is inherent in process
can one see that, although sorrow can originate in joy, joy
can also come out of sorrow. For the principle of beauty
exists in all things:

> to bear all naked truths,
> And to envisage circumstance, all calm,
> That is the top of sovereignty. (2. 203–5)

Although Keats knew all of this much earlier, he now affirms that his own spiritual development has proceeded to
the point where he can, like Apollo, become a mighty poet
of human agony.

Of all the Titans it is Mnemosyne who is most moved by
Apollo's songs, which she says are heard with "pain and
pleasure" both (3. 66). Mnemosyne's sympathy springs, one

supposes, from the fact that she is the goddess of memory. As the link to the whole world of the past, she would be perhaps more intensely aware than anyone else of the universality of suffering. That is certainly true of Moneta, her equivalent in *The Fall of Hyperion,* and Keats implores her in that poem to allow him a glimpse of her vast knowledge. "Let me behold," he says, "what in thy brain so ferments to and fro" (1. 289–290). In "Hyperion" this situation has two parallels, the first when Mnemosyne asks Apollo to "show thy heart's secret to" her, and the second when Apollo reads "a wondrous lesson" in Mnemosyne's "silent face" (3. 76, 112). The fact that in *The Fall of Hyperion* it is Keats himself rather than Apollo who stares at the goddess only confirms that Apollo does indeed stand for Keats. The more direct focus in *The Fall* on the process whereby Keats the poet learns from the goddess is consistent with that poem's increased emphasis on the maturation of the tragic poet.

In *The Fall of Hyperion,* Keats places even greater weight than he does in "Hyperion" on the presence of suffering and the need to face up to it both in life and in poetry. Although I do not undertake a full discussion of *The Fall of Hyperion* in this book, it will be valuable for us to remember that that poem, with its various rites of passage and unveiling ceremonies, in many ways resembles an initiation ritual. As such, *The Fall of Hyperion* places even more emphasis than "Hyperion" does on individual growth, so that Aileen Ward's suggestion that "the theme of *Hyperion* is the struggle of spiritual growth itself" is even more applicable to *The Fall.*[17] This, in fact, may be the most essential difference between the two versions: while "Hyperion" focuses primarily on historical development and its connection with poetry, *The Fall* deals with that issue at the same time that it deals with the question of personal development. As such, *The Fall* attempts a kind of synthesis of the insights concerning individual, historical, and poetic development explored in the "vale of Soul-making" and "Mansion of Many Apartments" letters.

Like many other critics, Ward believes that both of these poems indicate a major change in Keats. She even goes so far as to suggest that Keats "had become a different person from the man who had written *Endymion* a year ago."[18] Biographically, this may or may not be true; technically, in terms of their sheer poetic accomplishment and power, the two "Hyperion" poems do indeed indicate a major leap forward. But they do not reveal any fundamental change in Keats's view of life and poetry, and the critique of dreamers in the induction to *The Fall* is not, as Ward suggests it is, "a devastating indictment of [Keats's] own previous achievement in poetry,"[19] but an attack on the kind of poetry that either ignores suffering or transfigures it in the context of transcendent reality. Keats's early poetry does not, as I have shown, fall into this category, for it already included a proper understanding of suffering. It is not Keats's essential ideas that change, but his sense of his own ability to realize them even more adequately. The initiation ritual of *The Fall of Hyperion* celebrates not a fundamental change of direction in Keats's view of life and poetry, but the coming to maturity of a tragic poet who had known his goal from the beginning.

iii

"During the pain Mnemosyne upheld / Her arms as one who prophesied" (3. 133–34). The religion that Mnemosyne prophesies at the end of "Hyperion" is the new religion of beauty that the Olympians represent. But I must reemphasize that although in the allegory of that poem he identified the Olympian religion with his own, in fact Keats considered it as an actual historical phenomenon to be several steps behind his own in the "grand march of intellect." This point can be seen most clearly in "Ode on a Grecian Urn," where the new religion of beauty that Keats presents is set directly against the implicit religion of the Greeks depicted on the vase.

Now that we have seen how characteristic and significant is Keats's use of religious imagery, we can scarcely gloss over this poem's references to the sacrifice, the altar, and the priest. Keats looks back on this marvelous world, and its illusioned innocence, with a mild nostalgia not unlike that reserved for the Titans in "Hyperion." These Grecians move through their religious ceremonies unaware that, as "Ode to Psyche" suggests, the only gods reside in the human breast. Keats brilliantly distances the whole culture in history by describing the town, to which they can never return, as eternally silent and mysteriously desolate. These images, together with the reverberation of "slow time" (line 2) and Keats's treatment of the urn as a surviving artifact, a "Sylvan historian" (line 3) of an earlier, pastoral era, evoke a stark sense of the inexorable march of history, and suggest that we too can never go back to this innocence. Like Schiller, Keats fuses the concept of a historical fall from innocence with the idea of progress. The modern poet, says Schiller, should "not . . . lead us back to our childhood . . . the way back to Arcadia is closed forever."[20] Nor, for Keats, should we want to go back to such illusion, however blissful it may seem.

The scene on the urn itself is blissful indeed—too blissful, finally, for Keats. That is why he so carefully preserves, in his interpretation of the lovely scene on the Grecian urn, the dark underside of human experience. For even though the picture on the urn is purely pastoral and free from tragedy, the fourth stanza reminds us that it grew out of the human world of flux and strife and that the town from which these lovely creatures came is now desolate. Although the

lovers are poised in that supremely happy moment of unfulfilled passion, the lover can never, never kiss; he has *not*
his bliss; and his love is *yet* to be enjoyed. In the pastoral
world of the Grecian urn fulfillment is impossible: the song
cannot conclude, the bride cannot be ravished, and the
leaves cannot change through the seasons and display the
variety of their colors. The music of spring may be beautiful, but autumn, we remember, has its music too—and that
music cannot be played or heard by someone who is "all
breathing human passion far above" (line 28).[21] My point
here is not that the lovers' situation on the urn is seen by
Keats as unattractive, but that the sculptor who has created
this beautiful moment of intensity has expressed his tale too
sweetly by failing to emphasize the harsh realities which
Keats, in his cunning and self-consciously competitive fashion, carefully inserts in his own rendering of the scene. One
cannot emphasize enough the confusion that results from
failure to distinguish the sculptor's rendering of the scene
from Keats's own. The sweet pastoral picture on the urn
does, like romance, have a certain kind of beauty, for it celebrates moments of intensity within life. And it also has a
very real kind of beauty in its own texture. All poetry, Keats
believed, must be beautiful at this level; but the most beautiful poetry of all will be that which draws its materials from,
and never evades, the tragic reality of human life.

Keats's conviction that tragedy is more beautiful than romance does not imply a condemnation of romance any
more than "Ode on a Grecian Urn" implies a denunciation
of the sweet pastoral scene on the urn. Both the urn and
romance are beautiful and as such they are consolatory.
Keats does, after all, call the urn "a friend to man" (line 48)
even after he has recognized it as a "cold pastoral" (line 45).
Still, though the urn may "express / A flowery tale more
sweetly than our rhyme" (lines 3–4; emphasis mine), Keats's
poem is even more beautiful, because he places the sweet-

ness in its proper context by referring to several of the harsh facts of human life which the sculptor omits: "a heart high-sorrowful and cloy'd, / A burning forehead, and a parching tongue," and "old age" (lines 29–30, 46). By including these human realities, and by accentuating the desolation of the town and employing ambiguous negatives in the second stanza, Keats suggests that bittersweetness, not sweetness alone, is the most consoling kind of beauty.[22]

Explaining Keats's conception of the relationship between life and art has been among the major concerns not only of the present book but also of the criticism that has preceded it. In "Ode on a Grecian Urn" this theme receives its most famous, and also its most enigmatic and controversial, treatment. The relationship between the values of life and art is the most inclusive category we can isolate in the analysis of this poem, and it subsumes all of the many paradoxes and conflicts that critics have remarked in the poem—e.g., motion and stasis, flux and permanence, mortality and immortality. Among the numerous commentators who have seen in the poem a conflict or opposition between the demands of art and life, some argue that Keats takes his final stand on the side of life, and others that he comes out on the side of art. Still another group of critics contends that the poem finally reconciles the conflict. My own position, although it differs considerably from those of Gérard, Murry, Wasserman, and Patterson, shares with them the view that the real focus of "Ode on a Grecian Urn" is on the function of art in life rather than on any tension between the two, whether reconciled or unreconciled.[23]

To conclude that "Ode on a Grecian Urn" presents anything like an indictment of art, one would have to assume a far different conception of art's function and potential from that which I have attributed to Keats. The ode does suggest that Keats's own tragic art is superior to the romance of the sculptor. But despite the urn's limitations, it too has great value as art. It is true, of course, that all art is finally seen by Keats as neither preferable to life nor capable of extinguishing suffering. The cold pastoral of the marble lovers can never replace the warm, breathing, human passion of flesh-and-blood lovers, but neither can Keats's art do that. Yet this is no rejection of art in favor of life. Keats has simply not conceived the issue as an opposition. The recognition that the figures on the urn are ultimately lifeless does not diminish the beauty of the urn or its potential for human consolation. Although art has its limits, within those limits its value is great, and in this poem, as in his others, Keats tells us that art is finally "a friend to man": its function, that is to say, is consolation.

Failure to understand this limited but invaluable function has led some critics to interpret the odes in terms that seem to me as alien to Keats as any interpretation imaginable. H. N. Fairchild, for example, argues that the major theme of the great odes is "that, despite [man's] longing to find joy in a real world of human warmth, art is better than life and death is better than art."[24] What Fairchild fails to understand is that art and life are not opposed to each other in Keats's mind. Art is not seen as "better than life" in "Ode on a Grecian Urn"; art, like all forms of beauty, is rather a way of making life better.

Other commentators have argued that the inclusion of the desolate town in "Ode on a Grecian Urn" points up the limitations of art which, according to this view, become progressively more obvious to the poet as the poem proceeds, and climax in the exclamation "Cold Pastoral!" (line 45). But such a claim again assumes that Keats has posed a kind of conflict between art and life, whereas it seems to me more accurate, and more consistent with his other work, to see the desolate town as establishing the context in which art exists.

Not only does art originate in the transience of human life and joy; it is largely because of that transience that man needs art. The mortal, imperfect condition of mankind is both the source of art and the recipient of its soothing powers. Gittings seems to me absolutely right when he says that the town is desolate not just because its inhabitants have been frozen into art, but because they are "dead in some remote past," and that even in art's most ideal moments, it "contains reminders of the world of inevitable decay."[25] The town reminds us that art, like the gods, exists only for man.

Similar misconceptions of the relation of art to life and of aestheticism to skepticism in Keats's work have led to a now legendary perplexity over the final lines of "Ode on a Grecian Urn." The beauty-truth equation at the end of the poem embodies the crux of the relationship between aestheticism and skepticism, art and life, in such a highly condensed and enigmatic way that it is no wonder so many readers have been teased so far out of thought at such a crucial juncture.

There seems to be increasing agreement among Keats scholars that the standard text of the final lines of the poem should place "Beauty is truth, truth beauty" in quotation marks:

> "Beauty is truth, truth beauty,"—that is all
> Ye know on earth, and all ye need to know.[26]
>   (lines 49–50)

Without exploring all of the possibilities in the now famous debate about these final lines, let me simply indicate that, as I understand them, the urn says, "Beauty is truth, truth beauty," and then Keats says, "that is all / Ye know on earth, and all ye need to know." The word *that*, in my reading, refers to the beauty-truth equation which the urn has just made, and both *ye*'s refer to the readers or to all human beings.

To determine what the urn means when it says, "Beauty

is truth, truth beauty," we should recall the section of *Endymion* in which the hero uses the word *divine* to describe "fellowship with essence" (1. 778–79). At that point in the poem Endymion's conception of divinity is based on the transcendent, and so it is reasonable to assume that in that speech he does mean something transcendent by *divinity*. In the larger conception of the poem, however, Keats is attempting to redefine divinity, and it is precisely that new understanding that Endymion finally comes to accept. If Endymion means one thing by *divinity* in that early speech, Keats, as it were, means something quite different.

The same point applies to the famous words spoken by the urn at the end of the ode. If, as the rest of the poem suggests, the urn's perception is limited to the pastoral and thus lacks Keats's inclusive vision of the tragic, the urn must mean something very different by *beauty* and *truth* from what Keats means—something that, compared with Keats's view, is both naive and escapist. For in the traditional sense of these words, it is, as T. S. Eliot said, simply not the case that beauty is truth and truth beauty. Eliot, one recalls, considered the lines "a serious blemish on a beautiful poem; and the reason must be," he said, "either that I fail to understand it, or that it is a statement which is untrue. And I suppose that Keats meant something by it, however remote his truth and his beauty may have been from these words in ordinary use."[27] I would suggest that it is not an either/or situation. If one defines beauty and truth traditionally, as the urn would seem to, then Eliot is right in saying that the statement is simply false, and Keats would agree. But Eliot is also right when he says he may not understand the lines, for he does not seem to grasp the meaning that Keats, as opposed to the urn, attaches to beauty and truth. As he does with Endymion, Keats makes the urn speak a crucial insight without knowing its true import, which can only be seen in the context of the whole poem. If in *Endymion* a central task of the poem is to redefine divinity, in "Ode on a Grecian Urn" it is to redefine beauty and truth, which in these famous lines Keats tries to do by deliberately contrasting his understanding with the urn's.

Now *beauty* and *truth* are extremely loaded words, and they carry with them distinct metaphysical associations. *Real* and *semireal* are also loaded words, and they too have metaphysical associations. But we have already seen how characteristic it is of Keats to use either a metaphysical or a Christian vocabulary for decidedly unmetaphysical and un-Christian purposes. And that, I think, is exactly what Keats is doing here.

Truth, I have been arguing, is for Keats not metaphysical but human truth, usable truth by which man can live. And beauty is that which is life-affirming. By merging these categories so that they become identical, Keats is suggesting that what is life-affirming is that which we can live by, and that which we can live by is what is life-affirming. I state this as a tautology purposely, in order to emphasize the radical nature of Keats's identification of these two terms. There is only one question for him here: how can we find grounds for affirming life? By obviating the metaphysical issue traditionally implicit in any conception of truth,[28] and by humanizing the aesthetic issue of beauty, Keats characteristically shifts the emphasis to the only realm about which he can be confident: the human.[29]

When Keats says, "that is all / Ye know on earth," the statement is to be taken quite simply: human beings cannot be certain about any other truth than human truth. We do not know what is metaphysically true, only what is true in human terms. But this is the skeptical implication of the equation, and like most other instances of Keats's skepticism, the problem it poses here has its solution, which we find in the other implication of the equation: "all ye need to know." This is the consolation: the identity of beauty and truth is all we need to know because, in this post-Christian, Keatsian world, what matters most is that which will help us endure a life of suffering, that which will give us faith that life is worth living—despite the hard facts that passion goes sour, melodies fade away, and everything (like the spring leaves on the happy boughs of the real world) must pass. If truth is that which we can live by, that which will make us, with Keats, choose energy and life over despair, then beauty is the only truth man knows, because it alone is life-affirming and consoling.

In "Ode on a Grecian Urn," then, we have still another version of Keats's new religion of beauty—but beauty in the Keatsian sense I have defined. Beauty is seen by Keats as the only and best solution to the undiluted skepticism of "that is all / Ye know on earth"; thus the beauty-truth equation, when properly understood, expresses a certain holiness. "I am certain of nothing," Keats writes Bailey, "but of the holiness of the Heart's affections and the truth of Imagination—What the imagination seizes as Beauty must be truth" (*Letters*, 1:184).

But again the question persists: how can the human truth of suffering (as it is depicted in the third stanza, for example) be considered beautiful? And the answer is that it is not in itself beautiful, but must be made so. However attractive may be the prospect of being "for ever panting, and for ever young" (line 27), Keats knows that it is impossible, and he embodies that knowledge in the very tone of the middle stanzas, in which the undercurrent of tragedy is felt throughout. As a result, the mellow appreciation of the scene on the urn stops short of naive longing on one side and cynical resignation on the other. If art is "a friend to man," the best friend will be that kind which is most human, and thus itself has "a heart high-sorrowful and cloy'd, / A burning forehead, and a parching tongue." Yet there is the clear implication in the final words of "Ode on a Grecian Urn" that, far from condemning man to a bleak and irredeemably naturalistic vision of himself, the recognition of his essential human condition can be the cause for joy.

It is a tragic joy, an angle of vision which we have already seen at work in the "vale of Soul-making" letter, wherein Keats justifies suffering not in terms of some higher scheme but only on the human terms of the value of fully realizing our humanity. In this sense, it is better to complete and fulfill passion, despite the pain involved, than vainly to attempt to stop time, to escape from loss, or to preserve desire and passion forever. And it is better because it is the only way of achieving genuine happiness: it is more beautiful, which is to say more life-affirming. For all its sweet attractions, for all its seductively innocent charms, for all its beauty, the picture of the lovers on the urn is, as many commentators have pointed out, finally lifeless—like La Belle Dame, Lamia, the idealized nightingale, and the visionary Diana of Endymion's initial search. It "dost tease us out of thought / As doth eternity" (lines 44–45) because the pastoral vision of life is as illusory as the transcendent. Keats calls the scene (gently chiding) a "cold pastoral" not only because he has been reminded that it is marble, but also because it lacks a genuinely inclusive view of life. It is an idealized, not realized, picture and Keats ultimately affirms the fulfilled and fully realized life and art, which inevitably include pain, instead of the unfulfilled, which deceptively pretend to avoid it. Death, for Keats, is not desolation but completion, the fulfillment of mortality, the final stage, as it were, of soul-making. He knew this even in his darkest moments, as in "Why Did I Laugh To-night?": "Verse, Fame, and Beauty are intense indeed, / But Death intenser—Death is Life's high meed" (lines 13–14). And death with fulfillment of life is preferable, Keats suggests, to timeless desolation, to an unfulfilled life that would avert suffering and thus preclude the intensity necessary to soul-making and the perception of "beauty in all things."

Epilogue

In the preface to *The Mind of John Keats* Professor Thorpe tells us that his "study began and ended with that significant utterance—

> 'Beauty is truth, truth beauty'—that is all
> Ye know on earth, and all ye need to know."[1]

It was out of eagerness to understand these magnificent but enigmatic lines that I too have undertaken a study of Keats. Interpreting them within the context of Keats's work as a whole, I have tried to demonstrate that, puzzling as they seem, these lines represent a highly condensed summary of his most important ideas about life and poetry.

I have been arguing that these fundamental conceptions never essentially changed, despite Keats's remarkable development as a poet. He realized from the beginning of his career both the problem he faced—how to find grounds for affirmation and hope in the absence of metaphysical certainty and in the inevitable presence of suffering—and the solution to that problem, which I have been calling "aestheticism." We have seen how easy it is to regard Keats as divided against himself. Even his historicism seems to conflict with his claim to universal truth, and his insistence that suffering not be explained away seems to contradict his belief that suffering can itself be beautiful. But we have also seen that Keats's claim to universal truth comes directly out of his historicism, and that his discovery of beauty in the very depths of suffering does *not* constitute a theodicy. Keats's solution to the problems posed by his skepticism was perfectly consistent, so that even in the perplexing conclusion to "Ode on a Grecian Urn" we find a statement of skepticism ("that is all / Ye know on earth") which is resolved in the consolation that the identity of beauty and truth is "all ye need to know."

I can detect no conflict in Keats between the values of life and the values of art. Poetry could not, finally, provide salvation, but it could offer consolation, and in the post-Christian Keatsian world that task becomes an urgent religious duty for the poet. If there is any dualism in Keats it has the character of dialectic, not conflict: the dialectic of joy and melancholy, of beauty and transience, of great good humor and mortal darkness. It is a kind of spiritual equilibrium that we find in Keats: not a tension of conflicting impulses but a marvelously balanced sense of both the limitations and the possibilities of human life and art. It is this, above all, that we feel in the poetry. The bittersweetness, the sense of the interpenetration of joy and sorrow or beauty and tragedy, stem from a view of life that is courageously but never naively optimistic, that recognizes the extraordinary potential of human life but never forgets its anguish.

I have suggested that Keats intended this view of life to be understood in religious terms, and that failure to recognize this has been partly the cause and partly the effect of the widespread misconceptions about Keats's two fundamental impulses and their relationship. Bate is certainly right when he says that the subject of Keats's religious attitudes "cannot be taken up in isolation" and that the evidence must be "carefully considered in a context in which much else must be taken into account."[2] I have tried to take much else into account in this book, and in so doing I have discovered that the subject of Keats's skepticism and aestheticism cannot be taken up in isolation either, particularly in isolation from the religious context of Keats's work. An understanding of the one requires an understanding of the other. To understand the nature of Keats's religious views one must recognize that his aestheticism was related not to escapism, idealism, or the visionary imagination, but rather to his discovery of a new kind of spirituality in the intensity of beauty; and that from the beginning his skepticism was as radical as his concern with suffering was persistent. However, given the inevitable circularity of interpretation, such recognitions are themselves contingent on an understanding of Keats's religious views.

But for Bate, we remember, Keats's "poetry itself is . . . largely untouched by any direct interest in religion."[3] If Bate is right, then nearly all of Keats's most famous poems and letters must be filled with religious language and imagery whose function is merely ornamental or conventional.[4] But Keats, as the evidence we have been examining indicates, deserves a great deal more credit than that. Far from being a peripheral matter for him, religion was a major concern, and in many important ways his work represents an attempt to mediate his radically untraditional but still essentially religious attitude toward life.

I say "untraditional" in order to recall my earlier distinction between Keats's religion and traditional religion, whose distinguishing feature I take to be its belief in transcendent reality. One could, of course, deny the validity of this distinction and simply define all religion as Professor Woodhouse does in his elaborate study of its place in English literature. "The minimal dogmatic requirement," he says, "appears to be the recognition of a power, anterior and superior to man, which serves to explain to man himself and his universe, and to give a measure of meaning and guidance to his life, and which therefore becomes the object of his worship."[5]

According to this kind of definition, Keats's faith would

not be a religion at all but a replacement or substitute for religion; and there are, in fact, certain advantages in considering it as such. Keats did not, after all, develop any kind of systematic ethics based on his spiritual beliefs, nor did he try to establish for those beliefs particular forms of prayer, worship, communal rituals, or any of the other activities usually associated with religion. But Keats was not a systematic thinker: he had as little interest in working out such matters as he did in developing an institutionalized religion. His task was rather to give body and form to this "vast idea" of his, this new religious and poetic vision which, like Apollo in "Hyperion," was just then, he felt, coming into life. I think that the advantages of considering this vision religious outweigh the disadvantages, since Keats's purpose was to redefine the nature of spirituality, to tie it to this world and not some other, and to find grounds for an affirmation of life that would be genuinely consoling without violating his profound skepticism or glibly transfiguring suffering.[6] Keats's faith was not simply a religious surrogate, a "mournful cosmic last resort" (to borrow Anthony Hecht's wry description of Matthew Arnold's position in "Dover Beach"),[7] but rather a surrogate religion, based on profound if unconventional religious feeling and on a sense that this new humanized religion was consistent with the forward movement of history itself.

Whether or not one accepts Keats's assumptions about history, it is still important to take seriously his views on what has, after all, been among the dominant concerns of romantic and postromantic literature: the problem of faith. Keats occupies a crucial place within that specific literary historical context—a place which, once we recognize it, allows us to see him squarely within the line of development from Milton through Wordsworth to Wallace Stevens.

"Once . . . a particular course of development is expected,"

says Mandelbaum, "an absence of change, or changes occur-
ring in other directions, are considered as instances of stag-
nation, of retrogression, or as having been in one way or
another, aberrant."[8] So, for Keats, were the Augustans,
whom he describes in "Sleep and Poetry" as a kind of hiatus,
a "schism" (line 181), an

> impious race!
> That blasphemed the bright Lyrist [Apollo] to his face,
> And did not know it.   (lines 201–3)

Though Wordsworth claimed to "pass . . . unalarmed" Milton's Jehovah,[9] he only approached Apollo, but never ultimately embraced him as Keats did. Nor, I think, did any of
the great Victorian poets embrace him, though the problem
of faith had become for them a kind of crisis, epitomized in
Arnold's image of "wandering between two worlds, one
dead, / The other powerless to be born."[10]

It remained for writers like Joyce and Nietzsche and Stevens to give body to that new world:

> Supple and turbulent, a ring of men
> Shall chant in orgy on a summer morn
> Their boisterous devotion to the sun,
> Not as a god, but as a god might be,
> Naked among them, like a savage source.[11]

Stevens is affirming in these lines what Keats already knew
a century earlier: that Apollo is an intensity of our own
making, and that only when we recognize and embrace that
fact can he become a truly modern god, who will help us
choose energy over despair.

This "vast idea" was "clear / As any thing most true" to
Keats as early as "Sleep and Poetry" (lines 291, 293–94). He
knew what he was doing and he knew it early. In every one
of his major conceptions—of beauty, of truth, of poetry, of
knowledge, and of holiness—Keats took his bearings from

the only dimension of experience that he could confidently know: the human. His faith that it was all we can and need to know was the credo of his new humanized religion, and the cornerstone of his entire poetic enterprise.

Notes

Introduction

1. Matthew Arnold, "John Keats," in *Essays in Criticism,* p. 112.

2. *The Letters of John Keats: 1814–1821,* ed. Hyder Edward Rollins, 2 vols. (Cambridge, Mass.: Harvard University Press, 1958), 2:116. All quotations from the letters are from this edition and, unless otherwise noted, appear without alteration of Keats's frequently erratic spelling, punctuation, and syntax.

3. Douglas Bush, ed., *John Keats: Selected Poems and Letters,* p. xiii; idem, "Keats and His Ideas," in *The Major English Romantic Poets,* p. 233. Cf. idem, *Mythology and the Romantic Tradition in English Poetry,* pp. 127–28. In his most recent statement, *John Keats: His Life and Writings,* Bush inclines more towards the chronological schema of Bate and Stillinger, arguing that Keats sees "man's movement out of the world of illusion into the world of reality . . . as essential for the artist and for everyone alike" (p. 15).

4. This has become perhaps the most common view of Keats, and it is shared by Walter Jackson Bate, whose position is argued throughout his two major studies of Keats, *John Keats* and *The Stylistic Development of Keats.* Stillinger argues for a three-stage development, the first change coming in the winter of 1817–18 and the second in 1819, beginning with "The Eve of St. Agnes" ("The Hoodwinking of Madeline: Skepticism in 'The Eve of St. Agnes,'" *Studies in Philology* 58 (1961): 533–55, reprinted in his book *The Hoodwinking of Madeline,* pp. 91–93). Leon Waldoff, in a psychoanalytical version of this position, suggests that Keats's skepticism represents a temporary solution to the fear of abandonment, coming midway between his earlier "dream of permanence" and his later "acceptance of reality." See "From Abandonment to Scepticism in Keats," *Essays in Criticism* 21 (1971): 152–58. Clarence Dewitt Thorpe, in his extremely influential *The Mind of John Keats,* takes a stand that lies somewhere

between Bush and Stillinger. He finds tentative conclusions in Keats rather than a consistent pattern of thought, and while he sees Keats struggling throughout his career with conflicting impulses (e.g., dream vs. reality), he thinks Keats does indeed make progress in working out solutions to these conflicts.

5. What I shall be calling Keats's fully humanized religion should not be confused with the "religion of humanity," that aspect of Auguste Comte's positivism which in the last half of the nineteenth century developed into an institutionalized movement in some parts of the Continent and England and elicited the interest of many prominent Victorians, including John Stuart Mill and George Eliot. Keats's position prefigures a great deal of the "religion of humanity," but in many decisive respects it is radically different.

6. M. H. Abrams argues that only by reading passages out of context can we attribute a "religion of beauty" to Keats (*Natural Supernaturalism: Tradition and Revolution in Romantic Literature,* p. 429). H. N. Fairchild, similarly, argues that critics have wrongly ascribed to Keats "a religion of *ideal* beauty" (*1780–1830: Romantic Faith,* p. 499; emphasis mine) by misinterpreting Keats's statement in the *Letters:* "I have lov'd the principle of beauty in all things" (2:263). But if the phrase is used properly—i.e., a religion of *real* beauty—it seems to me both accurate and useful.

7. Bate, *John Keats,* p. 133n. Curiously, after explaining why —and apparently condoning the fact that—scholars have rarely pursued the subject of religion in Keats, Bate says: "Yet the subject, however elusive, has a considerable importance" (p. 133).

8. Robert M. Ryan, *Keats: The Religious Sense,* pp. 5, 23. Ryan does deal with a few of Keats's poems (e.g., "Written Upon the Top of Ben Nevis," "Written in Disgust of Vulgar Superstition") but he argues that "before one attempts to interpret the religious significance of the poetry, it is useful to have a fairly clear conception of the poet's personal creed" (p. 6). That, I think, is to put the cart before the horse.

9. Aside from Ryan's, the most valuable of the extended explorations of Keats's religious views is Newell F. Ford's "Holy Living and Holy Dying in Keats's Poetry," *Keats-Shelley Journal* 20 (1971): 37–61, in which he examines the ritualistic dimensions of Keats's poems and draws on analogies from the Christian

Mass to indicate the ways in which Keats gives "religious value and tone to the human condition" and especially to "his Supreme Mistress, Beauty" (pp. 38, 40). But Ford does not see the important implications of this view. Although he recognizes that the religious language is pervasive and that it is "not merely graceful metaphor or the 'dress' of wit" (p. 38), he never explains exactly what beauty means for Keats, and he continues to see Keats as involved in a " 'grievous feud' between . . . two mental worlds—the world of imaginative transcendence and the world of 'habitual self' " (p. 59). As a result, Ford's interpretation of the poems remains largely conventional. The view of Keats's religion that is closest to mine is Harold Bloom's, in *The Visionary Company: A Reading of English Romantic Poetry*, pp. 380–458. Although Bloom does not develop his observations about Keats's religious concerns, and although he sometimes wavers in his claims, Bloom does consider Keats a modern secular humanist. John Middleton Murry's rather complex view of Keats's religion is argued throughout his numerous studies of Keats. See especially *Keats and Shakespeare: A Study of Keats' Poetic Life from 1816 to 1820* and *Keats*. James Benziger's *Images of Eternity: Studies in the Poetry of Religious Vision from Wordsworth to T. S. Eliot*, pp. 103–37, presents an extremely balanced and provocative discussion of Keats's religious attitudes and their relationship to the romantic and postromantic traditions. Benziger deals incisively and fairly with both the orthodox critique of Keats in Fairchild's *Romantic Faith* and what Benziger calls the "modern humanist" view of Keats presented by Thorpe in *The Mind of John Keats* and Claude Lee Finney in *The Evolution of Keats's Poetry*. This "modern humanist" version of Keats denies that he was in any way a religious poet, and as such it is obviously quite distinct from the view of Keats that I present. Cf. Jacob D. Wigod, "The Meaning of *Endymion*," *PMLA* 68 (1953): 790n. Much remains to be said about religious themes in Keats, particularly in "La Belle Dame," "Lamia," "Ode to a Nightingale," "The Eve of St. Mark," and *The Fall of Hyperion* —poems which I discuss only very briefly.

10. Abrams, *Natural Supernaturalism*, pp. 12–13.

11. *The Poetical Works of John Keats*, 2nd ed., ed. H. W. Garrod (Oxford: Clarendon, 1958), p. 263 ("Ode to Psyche," lines 40–41). All quotations from the poems are from this edition. Hereafter, reference will be made only to the line numbers,

which will be included in parentheses immediately following the quotation in the text.

12. Murry, *Keats and Shakespeare*, p. 32. W. H. Evert also contends that Keats's ideas matured earlier than is generally believed. See his *Aesthetic and Myth in the Poetry of Keats*, p. 26.

13. Murry, *Keats and Shakespeare*, p. 5.

14. Murry, *Keats*, p. 15.

Chapter I — The Problem: Skepticism

1. Additional examples of Keats's religious skepticism occur throughout his letters, e.g., 1:319–20; 2: 51, 63, 70, 106, 304.

2. Hyder Edward Rollins, ed., *The Keats Circle*, 2:292.

3. Stuart M. Sperry, Jr., "Keats's Skepticism and Voltaire," *Keats-Shelley Journal* 12 (1963): 75–93. Although Sperry acknowledges the skepticism in Keats, he considers it part of that impulse in the poet that was in tension with the aestheticism: "The rational and skeptical strain may be secondary in Keats's nature, but it often acted to restrain his visionary longings, prompted self-criticism, and accounts for much of the tension central to his thought and poetry" (p. 93). In his book, *Keats the Poet*, Sperry says very little indeed about Keats's skepticism. While acknowledging that the second generation of romantics are trying to discover "a faith sufficient to replace creeds that have become manifestly outworn" (p. 246), Sperry identifies Keats's resolution of the problem with an irony that "is related to Shelley's habitual inability to choose, his recognition . . . of the irrelevance of choosing, between skepticism and 'mild faith' " (p. 245).

4. Robert Gittings, *John Keats*, p. 307.

5. Gittings and D. G. James have realized the extent of Keats's skepticism but not its import. James sees Keats's skepticism as inherent in the very nature of the human imagination, which, he contends, "can never hope to free itself of scepticism" (*Scepticism and Poetry: An Essay on the Poetic Imagination*, p. 9). This position, which James also develops in *The Romantic Comedy: An Essay on English Romanticism*, pp. 191–97, is certainly one that the first generation of romantics would have rejected. That Keats might well have accepted it is less a measure of its truth than of Keats's difference from the early romantics.

6. The word *metaphysics* has been and still is used in many different ways, even by philosophers. The meaning that I have in mind and that I shall be using throughout this book is "the study of things transcending nature—that is, existing separately from nature and having more intrinsic reality and value than the things of nature" (*The Encyclopedia of Philosophy*, s.v. "Metaphysics, History of").

7. Earl Wasserman, *The Finer Tone: Keats' Major Poems*, p. 8.

8. In 1818 Keats told Reynolds that "in about a years time" he would ask Hazlitt "the best metaphysical road I can take" (*Letters*, 1:274). But it is not clear either that he meant something beyond a general view of reality or that he ever adopted such a view.

9. C. E. Pulos, *The Deep Truth: A Study of Shelley's Scepticism*, p. 5; Franklin L. Baumer, *Religion and the Rise of Scepticism*, p. 77; Abrams, *Natural Supernaturalism*, pp. 68, 66.

10. Willard L. Sperry, "Wordsworth's Religion," in *Wordsworth: Centenary Studies*, p. 160.

11. In this regard I have found the controversy over Richard Brantley's *Wordsworth's "Natural Methodism"* very interesting. Though I disagree with Brantley's claim that Wordsworth is fundamentally a Christian poet, I can understand why he might have taken such a position. Even one of Brantley's harshest reviewers acknowledges that "phrases and passages and even whole poems occur before 1805—some as early as 1798—for which the prevailingly secular interpretation cannot easily account" (Alan Grob, "Richard E. Brantley, *Wordsworth's 'Natural Methodism'*: A Review," *Wordsworth Circle* 7 [1976]: 178). The problem lies in the assumption that the Christian and the secular are the only two alternatives. But I have been arguing that there is a third position, which more accurately defines Wordsworth, which lies somewhere between the supernaturalism of, say, Milton and the pure naturalism of Keats. It is obvious that by contrast with Milton, Wordsworth is very secular; it has been less obvious that by contrast with Keats, Wordsworth is considerably more traditional.

12. A. S. P. Woodhouse, *The Poet and His Faith: Religion and Poetry in England from Spenser to Eliot and Auden*, p. 164.

13. W. K. C. Guthrie, *The Greeks and Their Gods*, p. 52.

14. Bate, *John Keats*, p. 133. Bate does admit that the poem

"by-passes" the "recent promptings" of Shelley and Hunt, and that their influence is felt mainly in the language (p. 135). But he never indicates the nature of Keats's departure, probably because he regards the "heart of the hasty sonnet" as "extraordinary naiveté" (p. 136).

15. Gittings, *John Keats*, p. 110; Amy Lowell, *John Keats*, 1:235; Bush, *John Keats: His Life and Writings*, p. 35; Robert M. Ryan, *Keats: The Religious Sense*, p. 98.

16. Murry's and Benziger's failure to consider the radical implications of Keats's skepticism may stem from the fact that each is in his own way at great pains to relate Keats to a particular kind of Christianity. This is especially true of Murry. See, for example, the essay "Keats and Milton," in his *Keats*, in which he says: "Keats was not a professed Christian, while Milton was; yet Keats, I should say, was much more a naturally Christian poet than Milton" (p. 253).

17. Bush, *John Keats: His Life and Writings*, p. 35.

18. Ibid., pp. 211ff.

19. Aileen Ward, in *John Keats: The Making of a Poet*, suggests that in these last lines Keats "may . . . have meant the poetry which, half a century later, Matthew Arnold thought would replace religion as an interpretation of life" (p. 83). But Arnold's conception, though in some ways related, is really quite different from Keats's.

20. Rollins, *The Keats Circle*, 1:181. Cf. *Letters*, 2:368, in which Severn quotes Keats: " 'miserable wretch I am—this last cheap comfort—which every rogue and fool have—is deny'd me in my last moments. . . .' " Later, Keats told Severn: "I now understand how you can bear all this—'tis your Christian faith" (quoted in Bate, *John Keats*, p. 693).

21. Quoted by Rollins in *The Letters of John Keats*, 2:4n.

22. See Rollins, *The Keats Circle*, 2:293, where Bailey, in his eagerness to consider Keats a believer, substitutes "I have a firm belief in immortality" for "I have scarce a doubt of immortality," which were Keats's actual words. As for Keats's attitude towards the truth of proverbs, cf. *Letters*, 2:81.

23. It was probably Dr. Johnson's famous "Preface to Shakespeare" that inspired part of Keats's formulation of Negative Capability. Johnson criticizes Shakespeare for "that bigotry which sets candour higher than truth." *Candour*, as Johnson himself defines it, is "sweetness of temper; purity of mind; open-

ness; ingenuity; kindness" (Samuel Johnson, *Johnson on Shake-speare*, pp. 71, 71n). Keats seems to be expressing just the opposite view from Johnson. Of course there is more to the conception of Negative Capability than its unspoken premise of metaphysical skepticism. For a useful discussion of the relationship between Negative Capability and such important Keatsian conceptions as intensity, sympathetic imagination, intuitive perception of concrete objects, and the objective and characterless poet, see Bate, *John Keats*, pp. 242–61.

24. *The Daemonic in the Poetry of John Keats*, p. 239.

25. *The Iliad of Homer*, trans. Richmond Lattimore, p. 489 (bk. 24, lines 525–33).

26. Preface to *The Excursion*, line 55.

Chapter II — The Solution: Aestheticism

1. Failure to understand the importance of consolation for Keats is both the cause and the result of failure to see its connection with his conception of poetry's neoreligious role. For a more elaborate discussion of poetry's consolatory and religious function, see chapter 3.

2. Jack Stillinger, in *The Texts of Keats's Poems*, p. 94, says it was written "probably in 1814."

3. "Ode to a Nightingale," lines 52, 55; "Why Did I Laugh To-night?," line 14.

4. Lionel Trilling, "The Poet as Hero: Keats in His Letters," in *The Opposing Self*, pp. 36–37.

5. *The Marriage of Heaven and Hell*, Plate 11.

6. Preface to *The Excursion*, lines 40–41.

7. M. H. Abrams, ed., *The Norton Anthology of English Literature*, 2:647.

8. Earl Wasserman, *Finer Tone*, pp. 97–137; Stillinger, "Hoodwinking of Madeline," pp. 533–55.

9. Stillinger considers Keats's skepticism a reaction against his early trust in the visionary imagination, whereas I have been arguing that Keats never really trusted the visionary imagination and that his skepticism was evident from the beginning of his career.

10. Four essays on the religious dimensions of "The Eve of St. Agnes" seem to me especially useful: James D. Boulger, "Keats' Symbolism," *ELH* 28 (1961): 244–59; Harold Bloom,

"The Eve of St. Agnes," in *Visionary Company,* pp. 396–403; G. Douglas Atkins, *"The Eve of St. Agnes* Reconsidered," *Tennessee Studies in Language and Literature* 18 (1973): 113–32; Gail McMurray Gibson, "Ave Madeline: Ironic Annunciation in Keats's 'The Eve of St. Agnes,' " *Keats-Shelley Journal* 26 (1977): 39–50.

11. "The Circus Animals' Desertion," line 40.

12. "The Equilibrists," lines 43–44.

13. Wasserman characteristically misinterprets "proper pith," associating it with "heaven's bourne" or the "extra-human realm" of "pure being" (pp. 74–75).

14. Even in his love letters to Fanny Brawne, Keats often uses religious language, e.g., 2: 133, 223–24, 270, 278, 286, 293, 304. Cf. "Ode to Fanny" ("Physician Nature") and "The day is gone, and all its sweets are gone!"

15. Jack Stillinger, *The Hoodwinking of Madeline and Other Essays on Keats's Poems,* p. 88. Stillinger says that this view is given its most direct expression in "Ode on Melancholy."

16. Hyder Edward Rollins makes a point of observing Keats's curious use of *real,* but he does not fully explain its meaning (*Keats Circle,* 1:282n). Cf. Bate, *John Keats,* pp. 241–42; and Sperry, *Keats the Poet,* pp. 68–70.

17. Robert M. Ryan, in *Keats: The Religious Sense,* takes just the opposite view. "Without a belief in immortality," he says, " 'soul-making' is pointless: it is only from the perspective of eternity that the sufferings of an earthly existence can be judged as finally purposeful or beneficial" (p. 209). Ryan seems to me to miss the whole point: Keats undertakes an explanation of suffering that, unlike traditional explanations, acknowledges the uncertainty that surrounds questions of transcendent reality and immortality, and consequently "does not affront our reason and humanity" (*Letters,* 2:103).

18. William Hazlitt, "On Poetry in General," in *Lectures on the English Poets,* reprinted in *"Lectures on the English Poets" and "A View of the English Stage,"* vol. 5 of *The Complete Works of William Hazlitt,* p. 6; emphasis mine. Hazlitt is describing suffering as represented in tragic poetry, but for Keats the point applies to actual suffering as well.

19. Compare the last two lines of Keats's sonnet "Blue! 'Tis the Life of Heaven,—the Domain," in which, after considering various manifestations of the color in nature, he concludes: "But

how great, / When in an Eye thou art alive with fate!" (lines 13–14).

20. "Sunday Morning," lines 63, 88.

21. *The Poems of John Keats,* ed. Miriam Allott, p. 538. Harold Bloom also misses the urgency: "The admonition of the first stanza is against false melancholy, courted for the sake of the supposed oblivion it brings" (*Visionary Company,* pp. 432–33). One of the few commentaries that take seriously the issue of suicide here is that of Helen Vendler, "The Experiential Beginnings of Keats's Odes," *Studies in Romanticism* 12 (1973): 593–97.

22. Allott, *Poems of John Keats,* pp. 538–39 n. 1. Cf. E. C. Pettet, *On the Poetry of Keats,* pp. 303–4.

23. Abrams, *Norton Anthology,* 2:669.

24. Keats further intensifies the contrast by humanizing nature in the second stanza, in much the same fashion as in "To Autumn."

25. Miguel de Unamuno, *Tragic Sense of Life,* pp. 204–5, 211.

Chapter III — The Program for Poetry

1. Morris Dickstein, *Keats and His Poetry,* pp. 57, 248n. The debate continues about whether or not Keats intended to cancel these lines (1. 187–202). Jack Stillinger, in his important book *The Texts of Keats's Poems,* p. 262, supports the view that the evidence for deleting the lines is unconvincing.

2. Dickstein, *Keats and His Poetry,* p. 58. Christopher Ricks, in *Keats and Embarrassment,* also ignores the religious implications of consolation, but he does regard consolation as central to Keats's conception of the function of poetry. For Keats, he argues, "the deep and true consolations of art are made possible by a relationship that is indeed not mutual or reciprocal as are the deep and true consolations of human relationships." Nonetheless, the artist "comforts those he sees not, and this is the essence of art" (p. 191). Ricks avoids Dickstein's misleading association of consolation with escape, claiming instead that "Keats's concern is the responsible lightening of responsibility" and that what animates Keats's "garden of delight" is "a consciousness of responsibilities suspended (not abolished or ignored)" (p. 148).

3. Two further examples of Keats's concern with consolation,

from among the many in the letters, are of particular interest. The first occurs at the end of a letter to Bailey: "O that I had Orpheus lute—and was able to cha[r]m away all your Griefs and Cares" (1:182). The second example occurs just after Keats has copied out a new sonnet for Reynolds: "It is not matter whether I am right or wrong either one way or another, if there is sufficient to lift a little time from your Shoulders" (1:233).

4. Bate, *John Keats,* p. 125; Aileen Ward, *John Keats: The Making of a Poet,* p. 91. The relationship between revery and poetry is, of course, an issue in the poem but not, I think, the central issue.

5. "On First Looking Into Chapman's Homer," lines 11, 13–14.

6. "The word 'knowledge,'" according to A. C. Bradley, "usually with Keats, has the same meaning as 'philosophy,' namely, such reflection on human nature and life and the world as any thoughtful man may practice." ("Keats and Philosophy," in *The John Keats Memorial Volume,* p. 46.)

7. Ernest De Sélincourt (*The Poems of John Keats,* ed. De Sélincourt) and Miriam Allott, among others, have suggested that the object of attack here is Byron. For a summary of critical views, see *The Poems of John Keats,* ed. Allott, p. 79n.

8. For a brilliant account of Hazlitt's skepticism, which in many ways resembled Keats's, see John Kinnaird, "The Faith of the Centaur: Hazlitt's Sceptical Triumph over Scepticism," *Wordsworth Circle* 6 (1975): 85–96.

9. The parallel goes even further: just as Milton considers his Christian theodicy the highest truth, so Keats considers tragedy the highest truth. For Milton, the Christian explanation is more comforting than the pagan because it is truer; and for Keats, tragedy is more comforting than romance because it is truer. For an interesting discussion of the relationship between Keats and Milton, and especially between "Ode to a Nightingale" and "Lycidas," see Victor J. Lams, Jr., "Ruth, Milton, and Keats's 'Ode to a Nightingale,'" *Modern Language Quarterly* 34 (1973): 417–35. Lams argues that "Milton's presence can be identified in [the] transcendent nightingale-vision; and that in the poem Keats rejects the vision as false" (p. 433).

10. In a number of his letters Keats indicates that he regards offering consolation to his friends as an important function of letter writing. See, for example, 1: 303, 324. John Rowlett has

suggested to me that it was thus perfectly consistent of Keats to copy out verses for his correspondents in the middle of letters. That he did so with haste and without scrupulous attention to accuracy suggests that his major purpose was to offer his friends and relatives the same kind of consolatory beauty that his published poetry offered the public at large. After writing the verse epistle "To J. H. Reynolds," for example, Keats says that he wrote the lines "in hopes of cheering you through a Minute or two" (*Letters*, 1:263).

11. The undersense of tragedy can be seen in many of the early poems, e.g., "To One Who Has Been Long in City Pent" and the verse epistle "To My Brother George."

12. The most influential Neoplatonic interpretations of the last half century have been those of Claude Lee Finney (*Evolution of Keats's Poetry*, 1:291–319) and Clarence DeWitt Thorpe (*Mind of John Keats*, pp. 48–62, et passim). Two reactions against the Neoplatonic reading are Newell Ford ("*Endymion—A Neo-Platonic Allegory?*" *ELH* 14 [1947]: 64–76) and E. C. Pettet (*Poetry of Keats*, pp. 123–202). For a helpful compendium of the major criticism, see Stuart Sperry, *Keats the Poet*, pp. 91ff.

13. Rudolf Otto, *The Idea of the Holy*, pp. 112, 116; Paul Tillich, *The Courage to Be*, p. 156.

14. Sperry, *Keats the Poet*, p. 48.

15. Ibid., p. 56.

16. Ibid., pp. 40–41; emphasis mine.

17. Ibid., p. 93.

18. Keats may also have meant the word *proper* to suggest the inherent propriety or rightness of human beings' finding their own happiness not in anything beyond the human but by strict adherence to it. In this connection, the metaphor of nourishment reminds one of Keats's advice to the lover in "Ode on Melancholy" to "feed deep, deep upon [the] peerless eyes" of his angry mistress (line 20).

19. Finney, *Evolution of Keats's Poetry*, 1:319; Bush, "Keats and His Ideas," in *The Major English Romantic Poets*, p. 235; Evert, *Aesthetic and Myth*, p. 155.

20. Evert, *Aesthetic and Myth*, p. 162.

21. Abrams, *Norton Anthology*, 2:642.

22. Evert, *Aesthetic and Myth*, p. 106. While I agree with Evert that this is the basis of the allegory, I disagree with his interpretation of it.

23. Keats may also be suggesting that in a figurative sense it is better to search the earth for spiritual riches than to look upwards toward heaven.

24. Compare the similar wording in "Sleep and Poetry," where Keats describes poetry as "might half slumb'ring on its own right arm" (line 237).

25. Glen O. Allen, "The Fall of Endymion: A Study of Keats's Intellectual Growth," *Keats-Shelley Journal* 6 (1957): 37–57; Sperry, *Keats the Poet*, p. 106.

26. Sperry argues that in fact "Endymion is not apotheosized in Cynthia's visionary heaven. There is no ascension to the skies. The two lovers merely slip quietly away together through the woods" (p. 112). But numerous factors, especially the fact that they vanish "far away" (4. 1002), seem to suggest that he really is enskyed. If Sperry is right, Keats avoided the problem that I attribute to the ending. In any case, Sperry has in mind a problem quite distinct from the one I detect. For another argument that Endymion is never "ensky'd" see Charles I. Patterson, Jr., *The Daemonic in the Poetry of John Keats*, pp. 92–94.

27. There has been some dispute about whether "the old oak Forest" refers to *Endymion* (romance) or *King Lear* (tragedy), but most critics have agreed that it is the former. This reading is supported not only by external evidence (the letters I quote and the fact that Keats often uses *forest* to refer to romance) but by internal evidence as well. The word *fire* in line 13 refers to *King Lear*, consistent with Keats's assertion in line 7 that he must "burn through" the play. Although line 13 ("But, when I am consumed in the fire") sets up a syntactical parallel with line 11 ("When through the old oak Forest I am gone"), the word *but* implies a distinction between "the old oak Forest" and "the fire."

Chapter IV — Keats's Historicism

1. For alternative views of this matter see Walter Jackson Bate, *The Burden of the Past and the English Poet*; and Harold Bloom, "Keats and the Embarrassments of Poetic Tradition," in *From Sensibility to Romanticism*, pp. 513–26.

2. I quote from the King James Version of the Bible, which would have been Keats's source. In that version the word *man-*

sions is a translation of the Vulgate's *mansiones,* which in the Revised Standard Version is rendered "rooms." The OED also lists the following definition for *mansion:* "A separate dwelling-place, lodging, or apartment in a large house or enclosure." With Keats's use of the word compare Wordsworth's in line 140 of "Tintern Abbey."

3. The biblical version keeps the distinction between human and divine life carefully intact. See, for example, John 8:23, 17:16, 18:36.

4. For a brief but provocative discussion of what he calls "immanent teleology" in the romantic period, see Abrams, *Natural Supernaturalism,* pp. 177–79.

5. Ralph Waldo Emerson, "The American Scholar," in *Nature, Addresses, and Lectures,* p. 68. Keats's friend Bailey said that Wordsworth was a "Christian Poet" and that "Keats obviously . . . felt him to be" (Rollins, *Keats Circle,* 2:274). Robert Ryan quotes this passage from Bailey's correspondence, along with some passages from *The Excursion* (4. 10–24 and 6. 6–12) which leave no doubt that there was an element of supernatural Christianity in Wordsworth (*Keats: The Religious Sense,* pp. 146, 150–51).

6. Maurice Mandelbaum, *History, Man, and Reason: A Study in Nineteenth-Century Thought,* pp. 42–43.

7. Ibid., pp. 52–53.

8. Ibid., p. 55.

9. Ibid., p. 45.

10. Ibid., pp. 100, 52. Cf. Abrams, *Natural Supernaturalism,* p. 201. Keats may also have been influenced in this regard by Spenser, especially by *The Faerie Queene,* which develops intricate analogies between cultural and personal spiritual history.

11. Keats's movement from the realm of Flora and Pan to that of the agonies and strife of human hearts has often been considered a version of the classic Virgilian movement from pastoral to epic. Though Keats does follow this general pattern, the more important movement for him is the one I have been describing— from pastoral to tragedy.

12. Cf. *Letters,* 2: 130, 219.

13. Witness this comment to Reynolds in the "Mansion of Many Apartments" letter: "it is impossible to know how far knowledge will console [us] for the death of a friend and the ill

that flesh is heir to . . . With respect to the affections and Poetry you must know by a sympathy my thoughts that way" (1:277–78).

14. "When I Have Fears," lines 2, 4.

15. Kenneth Allott is one of the few critics who venture an explanation of the allusion; but his suggestion that the allusion underscores "a nostalgia for an imagined wholeness of being once possible" misses the nativity parallel between Christ and Psyche, and ignores the various indications of Olympian innocence. ("The 'Ode to Psyche,'" in *John Keats: A Reassessment*, p. 88. Reprinted in *Twentieth Century Interpretations of Keats's Odes*, ed. Jack Stillinger, p. 26). The lines I quote from Milton refer to the silencing of the oracles, which involved the displacement of the old gods—a tradition which Plutarch explained in *De defectu oraculorum* (*The Obsolescence of the Oracles*) and which elicited a good deal of interest in the late eighteenth and nineteenth centuries, primarily in Schiller's "Die Götter Griechenlands" ("Gods of Greece") and Elizabeth Barrett Browning's passionate response, "The Dead Pan." According to the tradition, Pan died on the very day that Christ was crucified. Compare Keats's "Hymn to Pan" and 4. 193–272 of *Endymion*. Other allusions to "On the Morning of Christ's Nativity" occur in "'Tis the 'witching time of Night'" and "Hyperion" 1. 350–53. For further parallels between Schiller and Keats, see note 20 below.

16. Gittings, *John Keats*, p. 185. Compare Robert Ryan's extremely illuminating discussion of the influence of Keats's medical training on his religious views. Most of Keats's teachers, Ryan says, combined "scientific empiricism" with "religious skepticism," and a suspicion of speculation with a belief in the necessity of observation. Their "willingness to accept uncertainty when there is not sufficient data at hand" and their "acceptance of, or at least patience with, incomplete knowledge" had a profound influence, Ryan claims, on the young poet (*Keats: The Religious Sense*, pp. 53–67).

17. Ward, *John Keats: The Making of a Poet*, p. 218.

18. Ibid.

19. Ibid., p. 328.

20. Quoted in Abrams, *Natural Supernaturalism*, p. 215. Although there are important differences, the parallels with Schiller are many and illuminating—e.g., the multiple developmental

analogies of poet, individual, and culture; the three stages of growth; the concern with the displacement of the old gods (see note 15 in this chapter). For a brief but provocative summary of Schiller, see Abrams, *Natural Supernaturalism*, pp. 199–217, 433, et passim.

21. The source of this famous line ("All breathing human passion far above") seems to be *Childe Harold* 2. 61, where Byron describes the isolation of Mohammedan women from their men's religious celebrations. The women, Byron says, are "joyful in a mother's gentlest cares, / Blest cares! all *other feelings far above!*" (lines 546–47; emphasis mine). It is no accident, I think, that Keats borrows from a decisively religious context.

22. The bittersweet sentiment appears with extraordinary frequency in Keats's poetry, most notably in "Ode on Melancholy" and "Isabella." In the latter poem, though the impulse seems to be to represent something beautiful growing out of a dark reality, the particular images Keats employs (basil growing out of a skull watered by tears) have created for most readers a bathetic effect. The bittersweet occurs in a great variety of other places as well, spanning Keats's career from beginning to end (e.g., "To Lord Byron," "Oh! how I love, on a fair summer's eve," "Sleep and Poetry," "I Stood Tip-toe," "On Seeing the Elgin Marbles," *Endymion*, "On Sitting Down to Read King Lear Once Again," "Welcome joy, and welcome sorrow," "Lines Written in the Highlands After a Visit to Burns's Country," and "What can I do to drive away"). Cf. *Letters*, 2: 133, 160.

23. Albert Gérard, "Romance and Reality: Continuity and Growth in Keats's View of Art," *Keats-Shelley Journal* 11 (1962): 17–29, reprinted in *Twentieth Century Interpretations of Keats's Odes*, ed. Stillinger, pp. 68–74; Murry, *Keats*, pp. 210–26; Earl Wasserman, *Finer Tone*, pp. 13–62; Charles I. Patterson, "Passion and Permanence in Keats's *Ode on a Grecian Urn*," *ELH* 21 (1954): 208–20, reprinted in *Twentieth Century Interpretations of Keats's Odes*, ed. Stillinger, pp. 48–57.

24. Fairchild, *1780–1830: Romantic Faith*, p. 492.

25. Gittings, *John Keats*, p. 320.

26. Jack Stillinger reaffirms this view in his important book, *The Texts of Keats's Poems*, p. 247. And H. W. Garrod, whose edition of *The Poetical Works of John Keats*, p. 262, prints the beauty-truth equation without quotation marks, includes them in his *Keats: Poetical Works*, p. 210.

27. T. S. Eliot, "Dante," in *Selected Essays*, p. 231.

28. If by *truth* Keats meant metaphysical or higher truth, the statement "that is all / Ye know on earth" would be ridiculous. For if Keats had metaphysical truth in mind, the knowledge that it was identical with beauty would be the kind of knowledge to which the limiting modifier *all* would seem inappropriate. What more could one possibly know? In fact, the force of "that is all / Ye know" suggests the *limitations* of human knowledge, the inability to know metaphysical truth. Albert Gérard's interpretation of *all* as " 'the best,' 'the utmost,' as in the phrase 'That's all I can do' " seems to me terribly strained ("Romance and Reality," p. 28).

29. As early as 1963 Karl Kroeber pointed out the humanistic emphasis in Keats's odes as a group—"The New Humanism of Keats's Odes," *Proceedings of the American Philosophical Society* 107 (1963): 263–71.

Epilogue

1. Thorpe, *Mind of John Keats*, p. v.

2. Bate, *John Keats*, p. 133n.

3. Ibid.

4. Bate clearly believes that this is the case with the early poetry, as his comment on "Written in Disgust of Vulgar Superstition" indicates: "Nothing could show more strikingly the subjective absorption in poetry into which Keats has fallen than the unintentional transference to poetry—or rather to *poets* (for it is with his powerful empathic identification with the great poets of earlier eras that we are dealing)—of terms, values, even symbols conventionally associated with religion" (*John Keats*, p. 136). In his discussion of the later poetry, Bate touches on the religious imagery but generally underrates its significance, especially in his analysis of "The Eve of St. Agnes" (pp. 442, 445). Bate would do well to remember Pope's remark in "An Essay on Criticism": "Those oft are *Strategems* which *Errors* seem, / Nor is it Homer *Nods*, but *We* that *Dream*" (1. 179–80).

5. Woodhouse, *Poet and His Faith*, p. 2. Robert Ryan also uses a traditional definition, which is similar, he says, "to this one taken from *Webster's Third New International Dictionary*: 'A personal awareness or conviction of the existence of a supreme being or of supernatural powers or influences controlling one's

own, humanity's or all nature's destiny . . . accompanied by or arousing reverence, gratitude, humility, the will to obey and serve' " (*Keats: The Religious Sense,* p. 6). For Ryan, Keats's religious views fit this definition.

6. In arguing that Keats's view of reality and understanding of suffering do not constitute a metaphysics or theodicy, I have been assuming definitions of metaphysics and theodicy which, in contrast to my definition of religion, are traditional. In fact, they are traditional in precisely the sense that I have attributed to traditional religion: they assume a higher reality. But to have distinguished between traditional and untraditional metaphysics or theodicy would have been misleading, since Keats was not attempting to redefine but rather to obviate metaphysics and theodicy.

7. "The Dover Bitch: A Criticism of Life," line 18, in *The Hard Hours: Poems,* p. 17.

8. Mandelbaum, *History, Man, and Reason,* p. 109.

9. Preface to *The Excursion,* lines 35, 33.

10. "Stanzas from the Grande Chartreuse," lines 85–86.

11. "Sunday Morning," lines 91–95.

Bibliography

Abrams, M. H. *The Mirror and the Lamp: Romantic Theory and the Critical Tradition.* New York: Oxford University Press, 1953.

————. *Natural Supernaturalism: Tradition and Revolution in Romantic Literature.* New York: Norton, 1971.

————, ed. *Literature and Belief.* New York: Columbia University Press, 1958.

————, ed. *The Norton Anthology of English Literature.* 3rd ed. 2 vols. New York: Norton, 1974.

Allen, Glen O. "The Fall of Endymion: A Study of Keats's Intellectual Growth." *Keats-Shelley Journal* 6 (1957): 37–57.

Allott, Kenneth. "The 'Ode to Psyche.'" In *John Keats: A Reassessment,* edited by Kenneth Muir, pp. 74–94. Liverpool English Texts and Studies, no. 5. Liverpool: Liverpool University Press, 1958. Reprinted in *Twentieth Century Interpretations of Keats's Odes: A Collection of Critical Essays,* edited by Jack Stillinger, pp. 17–31. Englewood Cliffs, N.J.: Prentice-Hall, 1968.

Arnold, Matthew. *The Complete Prose Works of Matthew Arnold.* Edited by R. H. Super. 11 vols. Ann Arbor: University of Michigan Press, 1960–77.

————. "John Keats." In *Essays in Criticism, Second Series.* 1888. Reprint. London: Macmillan, 1911.

————. *Poetical Works.* Edited by C. B. Tinker and H. F. Lowry. 3rd ed., 1950. Reprint. London: Oxford University Press, Oxford Standard Authors, 1969.

Atkins, G. Douglas. "*The Eve of St. Agnes* Reconsidered." *Tennessee Studies in Language and Literature* 18 (1973): 113–32.

Baldwin, Dane Lewis; Broughton, Leslie Nathan; Evans, Laura Cooper; Hebel, John William; Stelter, Benjamin F.; and Thayer, Mary Rebecca, comps. and eds. *A Concordance to the Poems of John Keats.* Washington: Carnegie Institution of Washington, 1917.

Barnard, Ellsworth. *Shelley's Religion.* Minneapolis: University of Minnesota Press, 1937.

Bate, Walter Jackson. *The Burden of the Past and the English Poet.* 1970. Reprint. New York: Norton, 1972.

————. *John Keats.* 1963. Reprint. New York: Oxford University Press, 1966.

————. *The Stylistic Development of Keats.* 1945. Reprint. New York: Humanities Press, 1958.

————, ed. *Keats: A Collection of Critical Essays.* Englewood Cliffs, N.J.: Prentice-Hall, 1964.

Baumer, Franklin L. *Religion and the Rise of Scepticism.* New York: Harcourt, 1960.

Benziger, James. *Images of Eternity: Studies in the Poetry of Religious Vision from Wordsworth to T. S. Eliot.* Carbondale: Southern Illinois University Press, 1962.

Blackstone, Bernard. *The Consecrated Urn: An Interpretation of Keats in Terms of Growth and Form.* London: Longmans, 1959.

Blake, William. *Blake: Complete Writings with Variant Readings.* Edited by Geoffrey Keynes. 3rd ed., 1966. Reprint, with corrections. London: Oxford University Press, Oxford Standard Authors, 1971.

Bloom, Harold. "Keats and the Embarrassments of Poetic Tradition." In *From Sensibility to Romanticism: Essays Presented to Frederick A. Pottle,* edited by F. W. Hilles and Harold Bloom, pp. 513–26. New Haven: Yale University Press, 1965.

————. *The Visionary Company: A Reading of English Romantic Poetry.* 1961. Reprint. Garden City, N.Y.: Anchor-Doubleday, 1963.

————, ed. *Romanticism and Consciousness: Essays in Criticism.* New York: Norton, 1970.

Bostetter, Edward E. "The Eagle and the Truth: Keats and the Problem of Belief." *Journal of Aesthetics and Art Criticism* 16 (1958): 362–72.

Boulger, James D. "Keats' Symbolism." *ELH* 28 (1961): 244–59.

Bowra, C. M. *The Romantic Imagination.* 1949. Reprint. New York: Oxford University Press, 1961.

Bradley, A. C. "Keats and 'Philosophy.'" In *The John Keats Memorial Volume,* edited by G. L. Williamson, pp. 45–54. Hampstead: The Keats House Committee; London: John Lane, Bodley Head, 1921.

Brady, Frank; Palmer, John; and Price, Martin, eds. *Literary*

Theory and Structure: Essays in Honor of William K. Wimsatt. New Haven: Yale University Press, 1973.

Brantley, Richard E. *Wordsworth's "Natural Methodism."* New Haven: Yale University Press, 1975.

Briggs, Asa. *The Making of Modern England, 1783–1867: The Age of Improvement.* 1959. Reprint. New York: Harper, 1965.

Browning, Elizabeth Barrett. *The Complete Poetical Works.* Edited by Harriet Waters Preston. Boston: Houghton, Cambridge Edition, 1900.

Burton, Robert. *The Anatomy of Melancholy.* Edited by A. R. Shilleto. 3 vols. London: G. Bell and Sons, 1893.

Bush, Douglas. *John Keats: His Life and Writings.* New York: Macmillan, 1966.

————. "Keats and His Ideas." In *The Major English Romantic Poets: A Symposium in Reappraisal,* edited by Clarence D. Thorpe, Carlos Baker, and Bennett Weaver, pp. 231–45. Carbondale: Southern Illinois University Press, 1957.

————. *Mythology and the Romantic Tradition in English Poetry.* 1937. Reprint. New York: Norton, 1969.

————, ed. *John Keats: Selected Poems and Letters.* Boston: Houghton, 1959.

Byron, George Gordon, Lord. *Byron: Poetical Works.* Edited by Frederick Page. 3rd ed., revised by John Jump. London: Oxford University Press, Oxford Standard Authors, 1970.

Carben, Edward. "John Keats: Pioneer of Modern Existentialist Thought." *Trace,* no. 55 (1965), pp. 322–32.

Coleridge, Samuel Taylor. *The Complete Poetical Works of Samuel Taylor Coleridge, Including Poems and Versions of Poems Now Published for the First Time.* Edited by Ernest Hartley Coleridge. 2 vols. Oxford: Clarendon Press, 1912.

Danzig, Allan, ed. *Twentieth Century Interpretations of "The Eve of St. Agnes."* Englewood Cliffs, N.J.: Prentice-Hall, 1971.

Dickstein, Morris. *Keats and His Poetry: A Study in Development.* Chicago: University of Chicago Press, 1971.

Dunklin, Gilbert T., ed. *Wordsworth: Centenary Studies Presented at Cornell and Princeton Universities.* Princeton: Princeton University Press, 1951.

Eliot, T. S. *Selected Essays.* New ed. 1932. Reprint. New York: Harcourt, 1950.

Emerson, Ralph Waldo. *Nature, Addresses, and Lectures.* Vol. 1 of *The Collected Works of Ralph Waldo Emerson,* edited by

Alfred R. Ferguson, introduction and notes by Robert E. Spiller. Cambridge, Mass.: Harvard University Press, Belknap Press, 1971.

Evert, Walter H. *Aesthetic and Myth in the Poetry of Keats.* Princeton: Princeton University Press, 1965.

Fairchild, Hoxie Neale. *1780–1830: Romantic Faith.* Vol. 3 of *Religious Trends in English Poetry.* New York: Columbia University Press, 1949.

Finney, Claude Lee. *The Evolution of Keats's Poetry.* 2 vols. Cambridge, Mass.: Harvard University Press, 1936.

Ford, George H. *Keats and the Victorians: A Study of His Influence and Rise to Fame, 1821–1895.* 1944. Reprint. Hamden, Conn.: Archon Books, 1962.

Ford, Newell F. "*Endymion*—A Neo-Platonic Allegory?" *ELH* 14 (1947): 64–76.

————. "Holy Living and Holy Dying in Keats's Poetry." *Keats-Shelley Journal* 20 (1971): 37–61.

————. *The Prefigurative Imagination of John Keats: A Study of the Beauty-Truth Identification and Its Implications.* Stanford University Publications, University Series, Language and Literature, vol. 9. Stanford, Calif.: Stanford University Press, 1951.

Frye, Northrop. *A Study of English Romanticism.* New York: Random House, 1968.

Gérard, Albert. "Coleridge, Keats and the Modern Mind." *Essays in Criticism* 1 (1951): 249–61.

————. "Romance and Reality: Continuity and Growth in Keats's View of Art." *Keats-Shelley Journal* 11 (1962): 17–29. Reprinted in *Twentieth Century Interpretations of Keats's Odes: A Collection of Critical Essays,* edited by Jack Stillinger, pp. 68–74. Englewood Cliffs, N.J.: Prentice-Hall, 1968.

Gibson, Gail McMurray. "Ave Madeline: Ironic Annunciation in Keats's 'The Eve of St. Agnes.'" *Keats-Shelley Journal* 26 (1977): 39–50.

Gittings, Robert. *John Keats.* Boston: Little, Brown, 1968.

————. *John Keats: The Living Year, 21 September 1818 to 21 September 1819.* 1954. Reprint. New York: Barnes and Noble, 1968.

————, ed. *Letters of John Keats.* London: Oxford University Press, 1970.

Grob, Alan. "Richard E. Brantley, *Wordsworth's 'Natural Meth-*

odism': A Review." *The Wordsworth Circle* 7 (1976): 173–78.

Guilhamet, Leon M. "Keats's 'Negative Capability' and 'Disinterestedness': A Confusion of Ideals." *University of Toronto Quarterly* 40 (1970): 2–14.

Guthrie, W. K. C. *The Greeks and Their Gods*. 1950. Reprint. Boston: Beacon Press, 1955.

Halévy, Elie. *England in 1815*. Translated by E. I. Watkin and D. A. Barker, 2nd rev. ed. 1949. Reprint. New York: Barnes and Noble, 1968.

Hartman, Geoffrey H. "Poem and Ideology: A Study of Keats's 'To Autumn.'" In *Literary Theory and Structure: Essays in Honor of William K. Wimsatt*, edited by Frank Brady, John Palmer, and Martin Price, pp. 305–30. New Haven: Yale University Press, 1973.

————. "Spectral Symbolism and the Authorial Self: An Approach to Keats's *Hyperion*." *Essays in Criticism* 24 (1974): 1–19.

Haworth, Helen E. "The Titans, Apollo, and the Fortunate Fall in Keats's Poetry." *Studies in English Literature* 10 (1970): 637–49.

Hazlitt, William. *Lectures on the English Poets: Delivered at the Surrey Institution*. London: Taylor and Hessey, 1818.

————. "Lectures on the English Poets" and "A View of the English Stage." Vol. 5 of *The Complete Works of William Hazlitt*, edited by P. P. Howe. London: Dent, 1930.

Hecht, Anthony. *The Hard Hours: Poems*. New York: Atheneum, 1968.

Hilles, Frederick W., and Bloom, Harold, eds. *From Sensibility to Romanticism: Essays Presented to Frederick A. Pottle*. New York: Oxford University Press, 1965.

Hirsch, E. D., Jr. "Keats's Aestheticism." Mimeographed. Charlottesville, Va.: University of Virginia, 1973.

Homer. *The Iliad of Homer*. Translated by Richmond Lattimore. 1951. Reprint. Chicago: University of Chicago Press, 1961.

Hulme, T. E. *Speculations: Essays on Humanism and the Philosophy of Art*. Edited by Herbert Read. 2nd ed. 1936. Reprint. London: Routledge and Kegan Paul, 1965.

James, D. G. *The Romantic Comedy: An Essay on English Romanticism*. 1948. Reprint. London: Oxford University Press, 1963.

————. *Scepticism and Poetry: An Essay on the Poetic Imagination*. New York: Barnes and Noble, 1937.

James, William. *The Varieties of Religious Experience, A Study in Human Nature*. New York: Longmans, Green, 1902.

Jeffrey, Lloyd. "Keats and the Bible." *Keats-Shelley Journal* 10 (1961): 59–70.

Johnson, Samuel. *Johnson on Shakespeare*. Vol. 7 of *The Yale Edition of the Works of Samuel Johnson*, edited by Arthur Sherbo. New Haven: Yale University Press, 1968.

Keats, John. *John Keats: The Complete Poems*. Edited by John Barnard. 2nd ed. Harmondsworth, England: Penguin, 1976.

————. *Keats: Poetical Works*. Edited by H. W. Garrod. 1956. Reprint. London: Oxford University Press, Oxford Standard Authors, 1970.

————. *The Letters of John Keats: 1814–1821*. Edited by Hyder Edward Rollins. 2 vols. Cambridge, Mass.: Harvard University Press, 1958.

————. *The Poems of John Keats*. Edited by Miriam Allott. London: Longman, 1970.

————. *The Poems of John Keats*. Edited by Ernest De Sélincourt. 5th ed., rev. London: Methuen, 1926.

————. *The Poetical Works of John Keats*. Edited by H. W. Garrod. 2nd ed. Oxford: Clarendon, 1958.

Kinnaird, John. "The Faith of the Centaur: Hazlitt's Sceptical Triumph over Scepticism." *The Wordsworth Circle* 6 (1975): 85–96.

Knight, G. W. "The Priest-like Task: An Essay on Keats." In *The Starlit Dome: Studies in the Poetry of Vision*, pp. 258–307. London: Oxford University Press, 1941.

Kroeber, Karl. "The New Humanism of Keats's Odes." *Proceedings of the American Philosophical Society* 107 (1963): 263–71.

Lams, Victor J., Jr. "Ruth, Milton, and Keats's 'Ode to a Nightingale.'" *Modern Language Quarterly* 34 (1973): 417–35.

Langbaum, Robert. *The Poetry of Experience: The Dramatic Monologue in Modern Literary Tradition*. 1957. Reprint. New York: Norton, 1963.

Lowell, Amy. *John Keats*. 2 vols. Boston: Houghton, 1925.

Lyon, Harvey T., ed. *Keats' Well-Read Urn: An Introduction to Literary Method*. New York: Holt, 1958.

Mandelbaum, Maurice. *History, Man, and Reason: A Study in*

Nineteenth-Century Thought. Baltimore: The Johns Hopkins University Press, 1971.

Matthews, G. M., ed. *Keats: The Critical Heritage.* New York: Barnes and Noble, 1971.

McFarland, Thomas. *Coleridge and the Pantheist Tradition.* Oxford: Clarendon Press, 1969.

Meinecke, Friedrich. *Historism: The Rise of a New Historical Outlook.* Translated by J. E. Anderson. 1959. Reprint. New York: Herder and Herder, 1972.

Miller, J. Hillis. "Literature and Religion." In *Relations of Literary Study: Essays on Interdisciplinary Contributions,* edited by James Thorpe, pp. 111–26. New York: Modern Language Association, 1967.

―――. *Poets of Reality: Six Twentieth-Century Writers.* Cambridge, Mass.: Harvard University Press, Belknap Press, 1965.

Milton, John. *John Milton: Complete Poems and Major Prose.* Edited by Merritt Y. Hughes. Indianapolis: Odyssey Press, 1957.

Muir, Kenneth, ed. *John Keats: A Reassessment.* Liverpool English Texts and Studies, no. 5. Liverpool: Liverpool University Press, 1958.

Murry, John Middleton. *Keats.* 4th ed. 1955. Reprint. New York: Minerva Press, 1968.

―――. *Keats and Shakespeare: A Study of Keats' Poetic Life from 1816 to 1820.* London: Oxford University Press, 1925.

Nisbet, Robert A. *Social Change and History: Aspects of the Western Theory of Development.* New York: Oxford University Press, 1969.

Otto, Rudolf. *The Idea of the Holy: An Inquiry into the Non-Rational Factor in the Idea of the Divine and Its Relation to the Rational.* Translated by John W. Harvey. 2d ed. 1950. Reprint. New York: Oxford University Press, 1958.

Patterson, Charles I., Jr. *The Daemonic in the Poetry of John Keats.* Urbana: University of Illinois Press, 1970.

―――. "Passion and Permanence in Keats's *Ode on a Grecian Urn.*" *ELH* 21 (1954): 208–20. Reprinted in *Twentieth Century Interpretations of Keats's Odes: A Collection of Critical Essays,* edited by Jack Stillinger, pp. 48–57. Englewood Cliffs, N.J.: Prentice-Hall, 1968.

Perkins, David. *The Quest for Permanence: The Symbolism of*

Wordsworth, Shelley, and Keats. Cambridge, Mass.: Harvard University Press, 1959.

Pettet, E. C. *On the Poetry of Keats.* Cambridge: Cambridge University Press, 1957.

Plutarch. "The Obsolescence of Oracles." In vol. 5 of *Plutarch's Moralia with an English Translation,* edited by Frank Cole Babbitt, pp. 348–501. Cambridge, Mass.: Harvard University Press, 1936.

Prickett, Stephen. *Romanticism and Religion: The Tradition of Coleridge and Wordsworth in the Victorian Church.* Cambridge: Cambridge University Press, 1976.

Pulos, C. E. *The Deep Truth: A Study of Shelley's Scepticism.* Lincoln: University of Nebraska Press, 1962.

Ragussis, Michael. "Narrative Structure and the Problem of the Divided Reader in *The Eve of St. Agnes.*" *ELH* 42 (1975): 378–94.

Randall, John Herman, Jr. "Romantic Reinterpretations of Religion." *Studies in Romanticism* 2 (1963): 189–212.

Ransom, John Crowe. *Selected Poems.* 3rd ed., rev. New York: Knopf, 1969.

Ricks, Christopher. *Keats and Embarrassment.* 1974. Reprint. Oxford: Oxford University Press, 1976.

Ridley, M. R. *Keats's Craftsmanship: A Study in Poetic Development.* 1933. Reprint. Lincoln: University of Nebraska Press, 1963.

Rollins, Hyder Edward, ed. *The Keats Circle: Letters and Papers and More Letters and Poems of the Keats Circle.* 2nd ed. 2 vols. Cambridge, Mass.: Harvard University Press, 1965.

Rossetti, William Michael. *Life of John Keats.* London: Walter Scott, 1887.

Ruthven, K. K. "Keats and *Dea Moneta.*" *Studies in Romanticism* 15 (1976): 445–59.

Ryan, Robert M. *Keats: The Religious Sense.* Princeton: Princeton University Press, 1976.

Schiller, Johann Christoph Friedrich von. *Poetical Works of Friedrich Schiller.* Vol. 1 of *The Works of Schiller,* edited by Nathan Haskell Dole, translated by Percy E. Pinkerton. London: Robertson, Ashford and Bentley, 1902.

Shakespeare, William. *Shakespeare: The Complete Works.* Edited by G. B. Harrison. New York: Harcourt, 1948.

Sharp, William. *The Life and Letters of Joseph Severn.* New York: Scribner, 1892.

Sharrock, Roger. "Keats and the Young Lovers." *Review of English Literature* 2 (1961): 76–86.

Shelley, Percy Bysshe. *Shelley: Poetical Works.* Edited by Thomas Hutchinson. 2nd ed., revised by G. M. Matthews. London: Oxford University Press, Oxford Standard Authors, 1970.

———. *Shelley's Poetry and Prose.* Edited by Donald H. Reiman and Sharon B. Powers. New York: Norton, 1977.

Sikes, Herschel M. "The Poetic Theory and Practice of Keats: The Record of a Debt to Hazlitt." *Philological Quarterly* 38 (1959): 401–12.

Simon, W. M. *European Positivism in the Nineteenth Century: An Essay in Intellectual History.* Ithaca, N.Y.: Cornell University Press, 1963.

Spenser, Edmund. *Faerie Queene.* Edited by J. C. Smith. 2 vols. 1909. Reprint. Oxford: Clarendon Press, 1961–64.

Sperry, Stuart M., Jr. *Keats the Poet.* Princeton: Princeton University Press, 1973.

———. "Keats's Skepticism and Voltaire." *Keats-Shelley Journal* 12 (1963): 75–93.

Sperry, Willard L. "Wordsworth's Religion." In *Wordsworth: Centenary Studies Presented at Cornell and Princeton Universities,* edited by Gilbert T. Dunklin, pp. 153–63. Princeton: Princeton University Press, 1951.

Spurgeon, Caroline. *Keats's Shakespeare: A Descriptive Study.* Oxford: Clarendon Press, 1928.

Steiner, George. *The Death of Tragedy.* 1961. Reprint. New York: Hill and Wang, 1963.

Stevens, Wallace. *The Palm at the End of the Mind: Selected Poems and a Play by Wallace Stevens.* Edited by Holly Stevens. 1971. Reprint. New York: Random House, 1972.

Stillinger, Jack. *The Hoodwinking of Madeline and Other Essays on Keats's Poems.* Urbana: University of Illinois Press, 1971.

———. "The Hoodwinking of Madeline: Skepticism in 'The Eve of St. Agnes.'" *Studies in Philology* 58 (1961): 533–55. Reprinted in *The Hoodwinking of Madeline and Other Essays on Keats's Poems,* pp. 67–93. Urbana: University of Illinois Press, 1971.

———. *The Texts of Keats's Poems.* Cambridge, Mass.: Harvard University Press, 1974.

————, ed. *Twentieth Century Interpretations of Keats's Odes.* Englewood Cliffs, N.J.: Prentice-Hall, 1968.

Thompson, E. P. *The Making of the English Working Class.* 1963. Reprint. New York: Vintage–Random House, 1966.

Thorpe, Clarence DeWitt. *The Mind of John Keats.* New York: Oxford University Press, 1926.

Thorpe, Clarence DeWitt; Baker, Carlos; and Weaver, Bennett, eds. *The Major English Romantic Poets: A Symposium in Reappraisal.* Carbondale: Southern Illinois University Press, 1957.

Thorpe, James, ed. *Relations of Literary Study: Essays on Interdisciplinary Contributions.* New York: Modern Language Association, 1967.

Tillich, Paul. *The Courage to Be.* New Haven: Yale University Press, 1952.

Trilling, Lionel. "The Poet as Hero: Keats in His Letters." In *The Opposing Self.* New York: Viking, 1955.

Unamuno, Miguel de. *Tragic Sense of Life.* Translated by J. E. Crawford Flitch. 1921. Reprint. New York: Dover, 1954.

Vendler, Helen. "The Experiential Beginnings of Keats's Odes." *Studies in Romanticism* 12 (1973): 591–606.

Waldoff, Leon. "From Abandonment to Scepticism in Keats." *Essays in Criticism* 21 (1971): 152–58.

Ward, Aileen. *John Keats: The Making of a Poet.* 1963. Reprint. New York: Viking, 1967.

Wasserman, Earl. *The Finer Tone: Keats' Major Poems.* 1953. Reprint. Baltimore: The Johns Hopkins University Press, 1967.

Wigod, Jacob D. "The Meaning of *Endymion.*" *PMLA* 68 (1953): 779–90.

Wilkie, Brian. *Romantic Poets and Epic Tradition.* Madison: University of Wisconsin Press, 1965.

Will, Frederic. "A Confrontation of Kierkegaard and Keats." *The Personalist* 43 (1962): 338–51.

Willey, Basil. *The Eighteenth Century Background: Studies on the Idea of Nature in the Thought of the Period.* 1940. Reprint. Boston: Beacon Press, 1962.

————. *Nineteenth Century Studies: Coleridge to Matthew Arnold.* 1949. Reprint. New York: Harper, 1966.

Williamson, G. C., ed. *The John Keats Memorial Volume.* Hampstead: The Keats House Committee; London: John Lane, Bodley Head, 1921.

Woodhouse, A. S. P. *The Poet and His Faith: Religion and Poetry in England from Spenser to Eliot and Auden.* Chicago: University of Chicago Press, 1965.

Wordsworth, William. *Wordsworth: Poetical Works with Introduction and Notes.* Edited by Thomas Hutchinson. New ed., revised by Ernest De Sélincourt. 1936. Reprint. London: Oxford University Press, Oxford Standard Authors, 1969.

Yeats, W. B. *The Collected Poems of W. B. Yeats.* Definitive ed., rev. New York: Macmillan, 1956.

Yost, George, Jr. "Keats's Early Religious Phraseology." *Studies in Philology* 59 (1962): 579–91.

Index

Abrams, M. H., 5, 12, 13, 37, 62, 104
Aesthetes, 17
Aestheticism. *See* Beauty
Afterlife. *See* Immortality
Agnosticism, 4, 14, 16
Allen, Glen O., 108
Allott, Miriam, 59
Anticlericalism, 9
Arnold, Matthew, 1, 16, 56, 162, 163
Art: function in life, 151–53. *See also* "Ode on a Grecian Urn"

Bailey, Benjamin, 7, 9, 10, 12, 14, 19, 21, 27, 28, 33, 48, 55, 57, 88, 98, 130, 156, 174 (n. 3)
Bate, Walter Jackson, 1, 3, 16, 71–72, 160, 161
Baumer, Franklin L., 12
Beauty: as alternative to Christianity, 28; defined, 28–29; function of, 29–31; not as escape, 32; as essential human truth, 34; symbiotic relationship with transience, 59, 61, 67; healing powers of, 59; melancholy as a kind of, 61; life-affirming, 5, 68, 155. *See also* "Ode on a Grecian Urn"; Principle of Beauty
Benziger, James, 17, 167 (n. 9)
Beowulf, 65
Bible, 18, 43, 116
Bittersweetness, 151, 160, 179 (n. 22)
Blake, William, 5, 13, 36, 57, 133
Bloom, Harold, 167 (n. 9)
Brawne, Frances (Fanny), 18, 32
Brown, Charles, 18
Bush, Douglas, 1, 2, 17, 102, 165 (n. 3)

Byron, George Gordon, Lord, 3, 79–80

Canterbury Tales, 43
"Chamber of Maiden-Thought," 43, 49, 145
Christianity: Keats's skepticism regarding, 4; Keats's antipathy to, 9; as myth, 15; Keats's critique of, 16; situation in modern world, 17; Keats's attitude toward, 18–19; humanized religion in opposition to, 53; its view of reason for history, 120–21; replaced by Keats's new religion, 138–40. *See also* "Ode on Melancholy"
Circe, 101
Coleridge, Samuel Taylor, 5, 11, 13, 34
Comte, Auguste. *See* Positivism
Condescension, 8, 71, toward Keats's early poetry, 6–7
Consistency in Keats's poetry, 7
Consolation: function of poetry, 30, 34, 84–85, 130–31, 156, 160, 173 (n. 2), 173–74 (n. 3), 174–75 (n. 5). *See also* *Endymion*
Critical interpretation, function of, 7–8

"Dark passages." *See* "Third Chamber of Life"
Darwinian thesis about nature, 15
Death, 32, 55–56, 57; "mother of beauty," 58. *See also* "Ode on Melancholy"
Deification: gods as a human creation, 35–36. *See also* "Hyperion"; "Ode to Psyche"
Despair and energy, 32, 33, 36

193

The Author

Ronald A. Sharp is associate professor of English at Kenyon College and coeditor of the *Kenyon Review*. He is coediting the Norton Critical Edition of Keats. In addition to his work on the romantics he has published translations of García Lorca and articles on modern poetry.